STUDIES IN ECONOMICS

J. Wilczynski   The Economics of Socialism
Margaret Capstick   Economics of Agriculture

in preparation
R. C. Tress   The Public Sector and the Private Sector
R. J. Ball   Macroeconomic Planning
Hans Singer and Caroline Miles   The Rich and the Poor Countries
A. B. Cramp   Theory and Practice of Monetary Management
I. G. Corina   Wages and Earnings
Ian Brown   Demography and Economics
A. P. McAnally   Economics of the Distributive Trades
F. S. Brooman   Money and Financial Institutions
K. D. George   The Structure of British Industry
G. A. Phillips and R. T. Maddock   The Economic Development of
Britain 1918–1968
A. I. MacBean   The Institutions of International Trade
R. D. C. Black   The History of Economic Thought
Charles Kennedy   The Distribution of the Product
Theo Cooper   Economic Aspects of Social Security
Gavin McCrone   Economic Integration
A. J. Brown   Regional Economics
W. J. L. Ryan   Demand
D. J. Horwell   International Trade Theory

STUDIES IN ECONOMICS

Edited by Charles Carter

Vice-Chancellor, University of Lancaster

1
Expectation, Enterprise and Profit

BY THE SAME AUTHOR

The Years of High Theory
The Nature of Economic Thought
A Scheme of Economic Theory
Decision, Order & Time in Human Affairs
Economics for Pleasure
Time in Economics
Uncertainty in Economics & Other Reflections
Mathematics at the Fireside
Expectation in Economics
Expectations, Investment & Income

Expectation Enterprise and Profit

The Theory of the Firm

BY

G. L. S. SHACKLE

London
GEORGE ALLEN AND UNWIN LTD
RUSKIN HOUSE MUSEUM STREET

FIRST PUBLISHED IN 1970

This book is copyright under the Berne Convention.
All rights reserved. Apart from any fair dealing for the
purpose of private study, research, criticism or review,
as permitted under the Copyright Act, 1956, no part of
this publication may be reproduced, stored in a
retrieval system, or transmitted, in any form or by any
means, electronic, electrical, chemical, mechanical,
optical, photocopying, recording or otherwise, without
the prior permission of the copyright owner. Enquiries
should be addressed to the Publishers.

© G. L. S. Shackle, 1970

ISBN: 0/04/330160/6

Printed in Great Britain
10 *on* 11 *point Times Roman*
by Alden & Mowbray Ltd
Osney Mead, Oxford

To
H. M. Boettinger

Editor's Note

Economics is a large and rapidly developing subject, and needs, as well as elementary works for the beginner, authoritative textbooks on special subjects. This book belongs to a series of such textbooks (more than forty titles are planned): the general level is that of the second or third year in a British university course, but the books are written so as to be intelligible to other readers with a particular interest in the subject concerned.

Those who study this book, or others in the series, must not expect to find an exposition of a settled body of Truth, which all economists must accept. Economics is not like that. It is at all times necessary to select, from the immense complexity of the real world, manageable sets of elements to study. This selection will rightly vary with time and place, and new insight will be given by authors who make their choice in a different way. An economics textbook trains students to think, in part by looking at things from an unusual angle. This book by Professor Shackle is an example: it is not the 'standard' textbook discussion of the decisions of firms, but it is all the more useful for the novelty of its approach.

C.F.C.

CONTENTS

PREFACE

The General Editor of this series, Mr C. F. Carter, has read my manuscript with that salutary critical exactness and penetration which, through more than twenty years, he has been willing, out of an extreme generosity, to give to a great deal of work of mine. If, in a number of cases, I have left my text as I originally wrote it, my excuse must be a difficulty which I have felt in departing from a scheme initially conceived as a unity, the expression of which I feel a need to leave intact to take its chance amongst such critical storms as it may meet. More than one person, baldly informed that the task of writing a book 'on the theory of the firm' had been entrusted to me, has been unable to conceal a hint of alarm. But the work on which the substance of this book is based is either the now wholly orthodox and long-established work of the value theorists of the last hundred years (Chapter 3) or of Professor Leontief (Chapter 2), or where it is my own (Chapter 5 and some themes of Chapter 4), it has been appearing in print, from time to time, through the last thirty years; so that its appearance in the present text must have been expected by those responsible for inviting this contribution to their series. I feel, therefore, that my conscience is clear. Chapter 6 deals with a region of theory which has been controversial since Cournot or Edgeworth. This chapter, again, incorporates some work of my own (*Expectation in Economics*, 1949, Chapter VI, on 'A Theory of the Bargaining Process'), but in highly essential respects it draws also on the admirable treatment by Dr Alan Coddington in his *Theories of the Bargaining Process*.[1]

I wish to express my very warm gratitude to Mr R. W. Farebrother for bringing to the reading of my manuscript a subtle and sympathetic critical sensibility and a rigorously exact standard concerning the mathematical expression of ideas. In verbal matters he has in many places suggested refinements, economies or amplifications of statement which have instantly commended themselves. He has been most generous of his time and care.

Mrs E. C. Harris has typed everything which here appears and has re-typed large parts of a chapter and many individual pages. She has been as always endlessly patient in reading my handwriting and ensuring a presentable copy for the printer's use. For all of this I am most grateful indeed.

The errors which may here be found are mine and no one else's.

For big business today the field of fiercest competition and the most glittering hope of success consist in the pursuit and exploitation

[1] London, George Allen & Unwin, 1968.

11

of novelty in products and technologies. The pursuit of profit has become the pursuit of knowledge. Thus competition, which has in the past been regarded as the mechanism of stability and repose, has become a self-energizing source of change. I dedicate this book to Mr H. M. Boettinger who, amongst the leaders of business on the very largest scale, has most brilliantly made this theme his own and has shaped from it an incisive original contribution to economic theory.[1]

G. L. S. SHACKLE

March 1969

---

[1] 'Big gap in Economic Theory', by H. M. Boettinger, *Harvard Business Review*, July–August 1967.

CHAPTER 1

The Nature of Production

1. THE MEASURE OF PRODUCTION

Part of life consists of enjoying things, part of it consists of making things enjoyable. The first is consumption, the second is production. The actions involved in enjoying our circumstances are likely, in themselves, to leave us with less enjoyable circumstances than before. A cup of tea can only be drunk once. Consumption destroys the enjoyability of things, production creates or renews it. Let us suppose that between two dates, say noon and midnight today, we do no consuming. Then the change we effect in our circumstances between those dates can be said to be production. Between these dates, some of the things, or parts of the quantities of things, that we possessed at the beginning of the interval would disappear, and other things would appear. If our efforts were well-directed, we should end with a set of things, or quantities, better adapted to serve our needs, more enjoyable, more useful, than we began with. If we could measure that increment of usefulness, we might use the resulting measurement as a measurement of how much production we had done. Some of the things we enjoy are such that their wastage does not matter. The air we breathe is replaced without any effort or sacrifice on our part, it is superabundant. Yet in a sense, of course, its usefulness is as great as that of life itself. We need to distinguish between the *ultimate* importance of things and their importance *in the circumstances*.

Measurement requires a unit, a standard thing with which to compare the things to be measured. To serve its purpose this unit must be invariant against change of circumstances, and must mean the same thing to everybody. These requirements may give no practical trouble when what is to be measured is such as length or mass, for these are the attributes of things only. But the *importance* or *usefulness* or *enjoyability* of a thing does not depend on that thing only but on the relation between the character of that thing and the desires and circumstances of a human being. We can perhaps, heroically, suppose his character and basic preferences to remain unchanged for the duration of our concern with him. But we cannot suppose his circumstances to remain unchanged, for it is only the effect of their variation which interests us. What unit measuring the importance

13

to us of the things we enjoy will serve for all varieties of things, in all varieties of circumstances, for all varieties of people?

The problem looks insoluble, and it is only solvable by a subtle and ingenious, though familiar, device. The *market* allows each person to adjust his circumstances so that the respective quantities of different things, which exchange for each other on the market, are agreed by everyone to represent his own judgement about their relative desirability. Thus price serves the purpose of a unit and a scale for adding and subtracting the importance of collections of various quantities of various things. Price, or market value, enables us to measure production.

One of the circumstances which determine how badly we want an extra weekly ounce of tea or tobacco is the size of the existing weekly supply to which this extra ounce would be added. The more ounces per week we are already assured of, the less it matters whether we get the extra or *marginal* ounce. Thus by reducing one item on the weekly shopping list, and increasing another by an equal market value, say one shillingsworth, we can adjust the relative acuteness of our needs for *small* extra quantities so that an extra one shillingsworth of tea just matters as much to us as an extra one shillingsworth of tobacco, so that we are, in fact, just willing to give up a shillingsworth of tobacco in favour of an additional shillingsworth of tea, and vice versa. As each person is able to adjust, in the same way, his own affairs to the market prices which finally emerge from all such adjustments taken together, we are all agreed as to how many ounces of tea are worth one ounce of tobacco. The price of tobacco is not, of course, usually expressed in tea but in shillings and pence. Nonetheless this money price is based on, and expresses, the universal market adjustment, or general equilibrium, in which everyone has brought his relative valuations of small extra quantities into equality with the relation of the amounts which can actually be exchanged for one another.

Multiplying the number of money-units for which each physical unit of some kind of stuff exchanges on the market, by the number of physical units we have on hand, we have the market value of our stock of that kind of stuff. Doing the same for each different kind of stuff that we have on hand, and adding together the answers, we have the value of our *inventory*. If, in some proper-named time interval (April 1971, or the week beginning July 14, 1968), nothing is withdrawn from our inventory for consumption, and nothing is added to it by purchase, and if we subtract the value of our inventory at the threshold of that interval from its value at the end, we have a measurement of the value which has been added to the inventory by production during that interval. Plainly, if there has been consumption or purchase, we can allow for these and still reckon the *value added* by production. Value added per time-unit is the measure of production.

2. THE NATURE OF PRODUCTION

Value can only be added to things by a change in people's desire for the things or by some change in the condition of the things themselves. Production is a change in the things themselves. It can be a change in location, shape, physical or chemical or biological constitution, arrangement in relation to other things, or date of availability. Any such change is inseparable from the notion of the passage of time. Any such change is *accompanied* by the passage of time. If a change of a given kind and degree occurs in a larger rather than a smaller quantity of stuff in a given lapse of time, we say that the measure of this production is greater. Or if a given kind and degree of change in a given quantity of stuff occupies a shorter rather than a longer time, again we say that the measure of production is greater. To measure production we have to consider the amount of change in relation to the amount of time. A simple form of production consists of change of location, as when natural gas flows out of the ground under its own pressure. The value added can be treated in this case as proportional to the quantity of gas involved. When there is no danger of confusion we can even speak of the gas, rather than its value, as being produced. The measure of production will then be proportional to, or represented by, the number of million cubic feet *a day* which flows out of the ground. It is plainly appropriate to call the movement of the gas a *flow*. But the essence of the matter is the momently coming into being of some state of affairs. In the case of the natural gas, the state of affairs in question is locational. In the case of the maturing of plants or animals it is biological. In manufacture it is a question of the taking-on of shape and being assembled. But in all these cases, by analogy with locational change, we can speak of a *flow*. In stating the measure of a flow we must say both how much change there has been (how much stuff has changed or how much change a given quantity has undergone) and also how long this change has taken. For the purpose of measuring it, production is a *flow*.

An object to which we assign an identity, such as a particular wheat-plant, may be continuously transformed through as many stages as we care to distinguish, of germination, growth, development and ripening of the ear. Yet perhaps it is better to think of production as what happens in a moment rather than what happens in a twelvemonth. In the motor industry, vehicles at every stage of fabrication and assembly exist side by side at any and every moment. By considering enough different kinds of component items and enough distinct stages of the process, we can see in the mind's eye the entire business of bringing a motor-car into being, from the metalliferous ores in the earth and the rubber latex in the trees to the final spraying of paint, as all telescoped into a single moment's comprehensive simultaneity. It is this composite picture, involving countless co-existing individual items each at a different stage or of a different kind, each destined to emerge in a different complete machine at a different hour or day in the future, which ought to represent for us the productive business as a whole, rather than the life-story of a particular machine eventually to be identified by a number stamped on its frame. Production is not to be thought of as a race starting at one moment and ending at another but rather as the *running* of a race, something which is in being at every moment. Nonetheless, in *measuring* production, we are in principle free to use any unit of time, long or short. The measure of the production that is going on is the ratio of the amount that happens, to the time it takes to happen. If we care to select a year as our unit, this will absolve us from difficulties when what we are seeking to measure follows an annual rhythm like the cycle of events on the farm.

To an observer who merely measured the quantities of the things visibly involved at any moment in production, it could appear in many cases that nothing was going on. The items of the list to which production adds value, and those of the other list, in which that added value is present, exist side by side in quantities which need not change. But something *is* going on. In each minute, day or year, some quantities of the things in the second list are drawn off and disappear in consumption, and are replaced by transformation of some quantities of things in the first list. This conception of two lists of items, one continuously or repeatedly engendered out of the other, is called an *activity*. Different technological stages or aspects of this total activity will be proceeding concurrently side by side at all times.

3. THE MEANS OF PRODUCTION

In the foregoing we have sought to define the meaning of production by saying how it is to be measured. To do this is to make of it an operational concept. Let us now look in more detail at what happens in production. The list of things which undergo transformation comprises two kinds of item. There are materials which are 'used up' in the process, which lose in it the physical or technological character with which they started. In contrast with these there are tools, that is, instrumental objects or systems which aid the process without themselves seeming to be changed in it. They range from the simplest hand tools to an entire telephone system. In reality, even tools suffer wear and deterioration, and in a long enough time are worn out or superseded and need to be replaced. Yet since materials are used up in a week or a year to a far greater value than the tools concurrently destroyed in processing them, it is useful to distinguish the two classes. Moreover, materials and tools do not by themselves suffice for production. Human beings on one hand, durable tools on the other, can be regarded as having something in common in their contribution to production. Each class provides a flow of services, and thus they modify the course of events without themselves being much changed. Services are of inexpressibly diverse kinds, and for a generally applicable concept of measurement we are perhaps reduced to supposing that every specimen of a given type of tool, and every human being exercising a given type of skill, makes in each time-interval of suitable length a contribution which does not vary from one member of the type to another of from one calendar-located week or year to another. Let us sum up the whole matter. Production consists of *activities*, each of which itself consists of *inputs* and *outputs*, or flows of materials or services contributed to or engendered by the activity. How, then, do individual activities fit together to form the total pattern of production in a society as a whole?

4. THE MATRIX OF PRODUCTION

Considered as one whole, the business of production in some society can be compared to a jigsaw puzzle. There is first the complete and given scene painted or pasted on a board. Then the designer of the puzzle is free to saw up the board into pieces which can be of any number, size or shape, provided only that they fit together so as to reproduce the original picture correct and complete. We as observers of the industrial scene are free to divide it in a great diversity of ways into distinct but interlocking activities. Each such activity can thus be made to include more or less of the whole scene, it can include many or few distinct outputs and inputs. Moreover, each output can be so specified as to have a greater or less degree of homogeneity. It can be specified, that is to say, so that specimens of the product selected at random are more or less nearly identical. Again, the inputs can be such as to leave much or little to be done to turn them into outputs. However, our purpose is to design the activities so that they fit together clearly and intelligibly into a picture of society's total productive business. For this we need activities which are in one-to-one correspondence with outputs. That is to say, we shall divide up the productive picture as a whole so that each activity has only one output, and each output comes from only one activity. The word *activity* is not ordinarily used in any special business connection. Accordingly it can be assigned an exact meaning of our own choosing, without this meaning being blurred and distorted by preconceptions derived from everyday language. If we wished to translate it into a single phrase of conversational and commercial usage, we should perhaps choose *an industry*. We shall, in fact, often allow ourselves to speak interchangeably of an activity, an industry and a sector. However, we ought no later than this point to consider carefully the relations of these words. An activity, for us, is properly something which goes on from moment to moment or from year to year. This word names the changing of things one into another, or one collection into another. That part of society, of the business and industrial community and of their organizational and material environment, which is occupied with some particular activity we call a *sector*. Since we are in some measure free, within the framework of technology, to design our activities and make them more inclusive or less inclusive, we are similarly free to choose what shall constitute a sector. In two respects, the use we shall make of *activity* and *sector* do not match the ordinary meaning of *industry*. In the first place, we have elected to confine an activity to a single output, while a single 'industry', such as the farming industry or the engineering industry, can produce a vast number of diverse objects. But secondly, in order to cover general production as a whole with few enough sectors to be manageable for calculations, we need to consider as a single output what is really a mixture of many different sorts of thing. The task of making these two considerations in some degree cancel each other, so that 'industry' can match 'sector', is one of the most teasing practical difficulties in studying production statistically.

Where do the materials and tools come from, that are used in an activity? These inputs of one activity are, of course, the outputs of other activities. Where do the outputs of an activity go? They may go direct to those who will use them for enjoyment, who will consume them. But they may go instead to other activities where, if they consist of materials, these materials will be further processed or will be assembled into other materials; or where, if they consist of tools, these tools will be used in production. Each activity is thus in general a nodal point or cross-roads, converged upon by many streams of products and sending out streams of its own product in many directions, to *final users* or to other activities. We shall see that this conception can be very clearly visualized by means of a square array or table of numbers, a *square matrix*, where each number shows the value of the product of some one activity which is bought in a year by some particular other activity. We shall leave the detailed description of this input–output table, and what can be done with it, for the next chapter. But its purpose and possibilities must be briefly indicated here.

A list of the respective quantities of goods, annually demanded by those who will consume or use them and not pass them on for further processing, is called a bill of goods for final use. The intricate and pervasive interdependence of sectors, each requiring, directly or via other products, some of the output of every sector in the society, implies that any change in the bill of quantities for final use will entail some change in the annual quantity required of the product of *every* sector. Even if the 'final use' quantity of only one good is increased, *every* sector will need to change its own output in some degree. But in what degree? This extremely intricate calculation is the main task of the kind of dissection, of the productive picture as a whole, that we have been discussing. Such an investigation is called *input–output analysis*.

5. THE DESIGN OF PRODUCTION

Until now we have been considering how the business of production can be defined, described and divided so as to obtain insight into its nature. We have said nothing yet about any influences that give it a particular shape, that govern or determine in detail what is done. Why are various things produced in this annual quantity or that? Why are inputs of such and such kind and size directed to producing such and such a product?

We saw in our first pages that in order to give the word production a meaning we had to describe a structure. This involved, first, the two inventories, the one to be transformed into the other with an addition of value. Secondly, we divided the goods composing the initial inventory into materials and tools. We listed inputs as comprising materials and services, the services being those of tools and of human beings. Lastly we asked what is the place, in the scheme of a society's production as a whole, of the notion of an activity in which a list of quantities of means of production is transformed into a list of quantities of goods made available per unit of time. In answer to this last question, we saw that the constraints on the specification of an activity are those of technology, which prescribes what can help to make what, and those of analytical convenience, which for the very important purpose of determining the list of total outputs required in order to obtain a given list of enjoyable outputs, requires us to specify activities so that each produces only one 'output'. So much for the bird's eye view of production in general and as a whole. Now we wish to look closer.

A policy is a list or system of principles by appeal to which we can answer the question what to do in this or that set of circumstances. The laying down of a policy requires only a general and loose conception of the type of situation which will have to be met. The policy may define broad classes of situations, and broad classes of actions, and establish a correspondence of more or less simplicity and explicitness between these two sets of classes. If the situations are envisaged more concretely, are felt to lie within narrow rather than wide ranges of variation, or are specialized to some particular environment or context of endeavour, we may prefer to speak of a plan rather than a policy. A policy or plan is the beginning of the practical expression of a purpose, and can be formed only in view of some purpose. The nature of the purpose bounds the choice of policy.

Purpose and policy are works of thought, and must evidently be the thoughts of some identified person or body, some distinct *interest*. When the policy concerns production, we shall call such an interest a *firm*.[1] The essence of the firm is that here production is *designed*. The firm is where the questions are answered: What to produce, how much of it to produce (in each week or year) and how (by what proportions of what inputs) to produce it. The concept of the firm is that of a centre of policy-making, of decision or policy-revision, and of management or policy execution. We have to consider what is the firm's purpose or scheme of purposes, what are the precise action-questions into which its general policy-questions must be resolved from day to day, what are the essential and what the contingent difficulties it encounters in pursuit of its ends, and what are the consequences of the leaving of production to be determined by the firm in its own interest.

6. REASON, KNOWLEDGE AND TIME

The method of economics is to suppose that men seek their ends by applying reason to their circumstances. By assuming that men will always do what is best for themselves, the analyst supposes himself able to predict their conduct as well as to account for it. In this procedure and argument there is one great difficulty, which disguises itself from us in our theory-making all the more easily because in our *practice* of the art of life and business we are for good reason tempted to brush it aside. This difficulty is that of knowing what our circumstances are. The source of this difficulty can be expressed in a sentence: Knowledge is about the past, but decision is about the

[1] Some prefer to speak of the *concern* in order to distinguish the policy-making and decision-making entity from the legal or technological entity. See B. S. Keirstead, *The Social Decision*.

future. This is the ineluctable 'human predicament'. There are no eye-witnesses of what has not yet happened or existed, and there can be no direct, observational, experimental knowledge of it. There is no means of *direct* knowledge of the consequences of our acting thus or thus. And at the heart of this general proposition we can discern one special logical dilemma which intensifies its force. Part of each man's circumstances, which should govern the choice of action he is now about to make, is the concurrent choices which are being made by other men. Can he wait, in any given matter of decision, until everyone else has made his choice and shown by his action what that choice is? Plainly this is not possible for *everyone*. The difficulty can only be resolved by an expressly organized *pre-reconciling* of choices. If men can offer each other lists of the alternative actions which each would take, conditional upon this or that set of actions being taken by others, it may be possible for a set of actions to be discovered, one action for each man, such that this is his preferred action given that each other man takes the action prescribed for *him*. This is the conception of equilibrium, to which a perfect market can somewhat approximate. But the kinds of action which can, even in principle, be thus pre-reconciled can relate only to the immediate future, the future so immediate as to be what we mean by 'the present'. For who would care to guarantee his course of action into that future where new knowledge of all sorts, actions in a context outside that of the scheme of pre-reconciliation, natural circumstances which cannot be foreknown, will prevail?

Like all humans, the businessman is the prisoner of time. If the act of decision or choice contributes in any true sense to the *making* of history, if it is an act of *origination*, then there can be no knowing for certain what will be the consequence of any course of action which he may now begin. For those consequences will be partly shaped by decisions taken in time to come, decisions which, we are supposing, introduce into the stream of history something that was not previously implicit in it. If decision is undetermined, the consequences of action are uncertain. But the businessman is not merely the helpless victim of uncertainty. He is at all times actively promoting it. For he hopes to discover and apply new knowledge, knowledge of natural principles or market possibilities, and in so far as knowledge is genuinely new it must subvert in some degree what has been accepted as knowledge hitherto. New knowledge is in part destructive of old knowledge. The businessman desires, and strives, to gain advantage over his rivals by innovation, by novelty in products or technology. The fact that a field for such innovation exists is itself a proof that business uncertainty is inescapable. Businessmen compete with each other largely by policies which directly create uncertainty. Innovation is the chief means of business success. There is in consequence a compulsion upon businessmen to search for possibilities of innovation and thus to bring about the continual evolution of society's productive system as a whole

Production looks to the future and sometimes to a distant future. Production consists of many different transformations of things into other things. But these diverse processes, though proceeding simultaneously in physical fact, are largely sequential and time-ordered in their purposes. The woollen yarn that is being spun today is intended to be woven tomorrow and cut into cloth next week. The cloth that is being cut today was woven a few days or weeks ago. What is more, the tools, plant and industrial facilities of all kinds which are being made today are intended to be used for years or even decades. Thus it is that choices and decisions concerning production can be only partly based upon knowledge, and must instead rely in vital matters and degrees on reasoned imagination.

7. TIME-HORIZON AND POLICY

Amidst his hazards the businessman has one comfort: The basic conditions are the same for all, he can reasonably hope to do as well as the next man, and where all are making some misjudgements, the average performance may be good enough for survival. He has also a number of methods of putting out of mind the knowledge of the insufficiency of his knowledge. He can argue that where the forms of future change are utterly unknown, it is sensible to ignore them and to assume that the existing situation will persist, at least for a time. For how long a time? The shorter the distance at which he elects to set his *time-horizon*, the more reasonable and the safer it may seem to him to act upon the supposition that there will be no important change. If that distance can still be sufficient for his productive arrangements to pay for themselves, provided this assumption of no important change proves to be justified, then a practical answer may offer itself: a particular horizon-distance will do, if it is near enough for what he knows of the present to seem to throw some light into the future, and distant enough for tools he acquires for production to give enough service to repay their first cost.

Although the businessman's problem is really indivisible, and the most advantageous course depends upon the whole circumstances whatever these may prove to be up to the most distant date which he deems ultimately relevant to his interests, there may in practice be no escape from the method of considering different aspects of his problem in succession, finding for each aspect many solutions, and at last selecting from each set of such partial solutions one which goes best with other partial solutions to form a comprehensive *policy*. In order to study each partial aspect of his total problem he must suppose some things known which in truth are only going to be discovered as the solutions of other partial aspects, or may even have to be invented in place of essentially unknowable things. If at first he considers a short enough span of the future, he can realistically take as given by recent history many circumstances which in a longer perspective are fluid and subject to be influenced by his own decision. For this *short-period* problem, enough may thus be assumed known to render the solution unique and determinate. To begin thus is to abstract certain elements from reality and make them into a manageable problem on their own, but it is not to be unrealistic. For in real life we constantly appeal to reason when reason has not, in fact, sufficient data to support any firm conclusions. Abstraction proceeds a step further. Even when they can realistically be assumed known, the data of the businessman's short-period problem are still an intricate mass of detail, the real detail of available technology, of the design and location of his particular existing plant, of his business organization and the personal qualities and potentialities of his actual managers and specialist experts, the tastes, habits and preconceptions of his potential customers. For insight into the basic logic of things, these particulars and accidental quirks of his situation must be encapsulated into more easily grasped and more distinctly manipulable notions, into *cost conditions* and *demand conditions*. Once a formal scheme has been understood, the task will still remain, even for the short-period problem, of rendering it applicable by interpreting its concepts and categories into terms of factual and quantitative detail. This will be a task for accountants and engineers and scientists.

The means of production, the inputs needed for the activities in which he is engaged or which he is proposing, differ widely in the speed with which the quantities available to him can be changed. If he is a farmer or a forester, his land cannot be extended without fortunate chances and long negotiations. A new design of industrial plant, indispensable for some newly invented process, will take months to build even when the site has been found, legal formalities completed and the design created on the drawing board. But larger flows of materials may be arranged overnight, extra labour can perhaps be collected in a day or two. For the economist, the *short period* means some length of time in which some of the circumstances of production which confront the firm remain virtually unalterable and beyond its control. These circumstances may evidently have been of the firm's own choosing in the past. Who fixed them is irrelevant. Only the future is *now* the subject of choice and decision.

8. MARKETS AND PRICES

This natural dichotomy of the firm's affairs into cost conditions and demand conditions is reflected in the traditional mode of economic analysis. In this mode the demand and supply sides of the market are first described independently of each other and then confronted with each other in order to discover a price which, if it were higher, would elicit more offers for sale than purchase, and if it were lower, would bring out more demand than supply. This approach not only lends itself to simple algebraic or diagrammatic treatment, but no doubt refers us to the basic conditions which determine the allocation of resources to this or that line of production. Things are high-priced when they are scarce; to say they are scarce is to say they are much sought after; they are much sought after when *two* things are true of them, that they are very much wanted and that there are severe obstacles to be overcome in getting them. These basic conditions may or may not be very much affected by the kinds of effort gathered under the word 'marketing'. At any rate the traditional method provides essential insights which the study of selling effort and advertising do not render obsolete.

In this traditional analysis the firm is conceived as the supplier of a single homogeneous commodity. It is free to decide either how many physical units per unit of time it shall offer (its output) or how many money units per physical unit of product it shall charge (its price) but not both, the price which can be charged depending on the output that the firm is resolved to sell. The precise character of this function (in the mathematical sense) connecting price and output is shaped by the conditions of the market in two respects: the numbers and attitudes of the potential buyers, and the numbers and policies of the rival suppliers. Thus circumscribed, the theory of the firm was created by Augustin Cournot, the first great mathematical economist, in his book of 1838.[2] It is usual nowadays to recognize five distinct sets of conditions under which the firm may have to sell. It may, in the first place, be the sole producer of a commodity which is in some respect peculiar to it, or is so regarded by the potential buyers: the firm may be a *monopolist*. Secondly, while still the sole seller of a product which in strictness is unique, it may be surrounded with other firms whose products are, in some sense, fairly good substitutes for its own, in the eyes and judgement of the potential buyers. If these other firms are evenly sized enough and numerous enough and, all taken together, do a large enough trade in comparison with our own firm, no one of them will be noticeably affected in the selling of its own product by anything that our firm does in respect of price

[2] *Recherches sur les principes mathématiques de la théorie des richesses.*

and output. Thus these other firms constitute a non-reacting environment for our firm's sales policy, a background which may of course change spontaneously, but will not change in mere response to our own firm's conduct. In this case, our firm will be engaged in *monopolistic competition*. Thirdly, these firms may be few instead of many, so few that each feels distinctly, in the behaviour of its own volume of sales at a given price, the effect of any change of price–output policy by our own firm. The firms, including our own, which compose the 'industry', are in this case *oligopolists*. If their respective products differ somewhat from each other, in physical character or design, in packaging, mode of sale or location of source, the situation is one of *oligopoly with product differentiation*. Fourthly, such a group of oligopolists may sell products which all potential buyers treat as identical with each other, and this is *oligopoly without product differentiation*. Fifthly, a product which, to all potential buyers, seems perfectly uniform and unvarying from firm to firm may be offered by vast numbers of firms no one of which is large in relation to the industry as a whole. This is *perfect competition*.

The important difference is between those situations where other firms will, and those where they will not, expressly react to what our firm does. No firm is free from rival sellers, for if it sets its price too high there is always something else on which the buyer can spend his money. All monopolists, we may say, are monopolistic competitors. Again perfect competition is rarely feasible in practice, if only for the reason that firms are differently located. Fishermen returning to port at the same time, and wheat-farmers in North America, may perhaps count as examples of it. For our purpose of insight, the difference between the many-competitors market and the few-competitors market is what matters, for they lend themselves to entirely different modes of analysis. In the former we can in principle express the demand conditions facing our firm at some named epoch, say May 1968, by means of a curve, or its equation, whose shape stays the same no matter what price per unit our firm decides to charge or, alternatively, what number of units per week it decides to thrust upon the market. By choosing an appropriate price the firm can place itself at any point on the curve, that is, it can sell, within a certain range, any quantity per week it likes. But when there is only a handful of firms producing some technologically defined class of objects, so that each one of these firms has a considerable share of the market, no one of them can substantially lower its price, and thus increase its sales, without noticeably biting into the sales of the other firms. When these other firms respond by lowering their own prices, the newly gained customers will flow away again from our firm, to an extent depending, not merely on what our firm has done or plans to do, but on what the other firms do, in respects which are quite outside our firm's control. Because there is no knowing how its rivals will respond, and because it will be as much affected by their response as they are by its action, the pairing off of each price which might be charged, with one and only one weekly quantity which would then be sold, and vice versa, is not possible. On the contrary, the duopoly or oligopoly situation (*two*, or a *few*, sellers) is highly paradoxical, almost necessarily involving one or other of the rival firms in wrong assumptions about its rival's reactions to any act of its own. Thus the analysis of duopoly or oligopoly must invoke entirely different methods from the *equilibrium* conception appropriate to a many-seller market. The 1970s and after is the era of few and huge firms in many industries. Such firms are not engaged in using price and output adjustments alone in adaptation to the small shifts of a stable and neutral environment. They are contestants attacking each other's markets with immense expenditures on selling effort and, above all, by ceaseless search for innovations of technology and product. These are the firms whose theory is required today. Nonetheless, there is a logic of markets discovered by Cournot, to which even they are in some sense subject.

9. THE PURPOSE OF THE FIRM

As economists we regard the firm as a policy-making centre controlling a productive activity. Production consists in buying inputs, effecting technological transformations, and selling the resulting outputs. A policy can be formed only in relation to a purpose. What objective does the firm pursue? So long as the firm is to serve as the essential building block of the free enterprise system of economic life, its purpose has to be to make as large as it can the excess, calculated according to some one of many possible schemes, of the value of its outputs over the cost of its inputs. When it abandons this purpose, it ceases to be a firm and becomes a department of state or an element in a syndicalist system or part of a totally centralized economic society. In identifying the firm with the free enterprise system, we do not involve ourselves in any judgement of relative merit, but merely seek clear distinctions. We are here concerned to discuss the firm and we must give this idea as exact a form as we can. If we wish to assume that the firm's conduct is intelligible, we are bound to assume that that conduct is internally coherent. To be coherent it will, in practice, need to set itself a single overriding purpose. It is natural for us to take as that purpose the one which corresponds to the firm's role in a certain form of society. We accordingly suppose that the firm seeks to maximize its wealth.

But this phrase is hardly more than an empty husk into which we still have to pour some content. Comparison is an act of thought, and takes place at some one, nameable, moment. The things compared are seen from that moment, and judged in the individual's intellectual circumstances and intellectual posture of that moment, they are judged in the light of what he then desires, knows and imagines as possible. Situations and occurrences which he imagines and locates in his future will not be treated and valued by him as though they existed *now*, in his present. Their valuation will depend on their own *form* (the picture which exists in the individual's thought), on the *deferment* into future time of the date to which he assigns that picture and on their *standing* or the degree to which he accepts them as serious possibilities and as *able to come true*. When such a conceived occurrence is the receipt of a sum of money, he will need to ask himself what sum of spot cash available to him now could guarantee to him the availability of the supposed deferred sum at the date to which he is assigning it; and whether he regards the receipt of that deferred sum as certain, or if not, what sum, *certain* to be then received, he would accept in exchange for the uncertain prospect of the sum in question. These two adjustments to the supposed deferred sum, on account of the distance of its date and the uncertainty of its realization, must of course be combined into a single operation, the operation of *discounting*, so that both take effect together.

A bond is a borrower's promise to pay stated amounts at stated future dates in return for the sum of spot cash which the lender hands to him today. There is a market where such bonds, created on the spot or existing from an earlier day, can be bought by a lender as his act of lending and sold by a borrower as his act of borrowing, or sold by a former lender who now wishes to regain such money as he may out of a former transaction of lending. When a new bond is created and a new loan made, the total of promised future payments is greater than the principal which is now parted with by the lender. The reason for this we shall see in Chapter 4. The purpose of the market is to settle at each moment the precise relationship between the series of dated future payments and the present principal. Such a relationship can always be expressed by means of some proper fraction, say $1/5$ or $1/10$, let us call it in general r, which enters into the expression $1/(1+r)$ by which every promised deferred sum is to be multiplied as many times as there are years in its deferment. When this operation of *discounting* has been performed on each of the deferred payments, and the results are all added together, the total, by suitable choice of r, can be made equal to the principal lent today. This proper fraction r is the *rate of interest* per annum prevailing in the bond market (the loan market) today. The existence of a market for loans implies that for the individual person or firm, there is at any moment an objective ratio of exchange between money in hand now, and money due at some specified deferment. The number of money units due in a year's time, or ten years' time, the promise of which can be had or must be given in exchange for one hundred units of spot cash, is for the individual businessman as much a fact as the thermometer reading. Such facts must accordingly be built into any production plan which the businessman may be supposed to design. The other aspect of his planning is more important still, and far more difficult to accommodate. The inescapable and perhaps wide-ranging plurality of the ideas which he can plausibly form about the sale-proceeds of future outputs and the expense of future inputs can be dealt with only by his own judgement. It may be best for the analyst to suppose that many variant plans are formed, each embodying one number and one only for the size or price of any (dated) input or output, but each resting its choice of this table of numbers on a different conception of the course of evolution of the business environment (the 'state of the world' at a series of future dates). Each production plan, in the set of rival variants, will thus consist of 'single-valued expectations'. Before we can consider the logic of the production plan, we must consider what will be the firm's means of action, since the extent of these means constrains the plan.

The firm's *fortune* at any moment comprises the market value at that moment of all the material objects and legal rights which it then possesses, plus the money it has, plus the debts owed to it less those it owes to others. Its *resources* at that moment consist of its fortune plus the largest total of debt it could then become liable for. Economic theoreticians have often assumed that the firm's borrowing power is limitless. There are several objections to this analytical practice. It confines the study of the firm more narrowly than need be to its treatment in isolation from the rest of the economic system. It is plainly not meaningful to suppose that all firms simultaneously can borrow unlimited sums. If they all did so, and attempted to spend the proceeds, the meaning and value of money would be destroyed. Thus a firm with unlimited borrowing power is something existing in a conceptual vacuum. But unlimited borrowing power is also at odds with observation. As a firm's borrowings come to represent a larger and larger proportion of its resources, lending to it (as we shall see in precise terms below) becomes more and more risky. The cost to it of borrowing a still further sum will therefore at some point become greater than any profit which the use of that sum in the firm's business could be expected to earn. Beyond that point, borrowing does not pay the firm, nor will potential lenders consent to it.

28

10. THE FIRM'S PRODUCTION PLAN

The policy or scheme which the firm proposes to itself, according to which it will buy inputs, transform them by combining them in technological activities, and then sell the resulting outputs, must reckon with market facts. Amongst these facts are the interest rates prevailing, for various lengths of deferment, at the time when the plan is being made, and the market's valuation, at that time, of the firm's material and intangible possessions. But these facts are merely a base from which its expeditions of imagination can set out to explore conceptually its possibilities of action. The relevant and essential value of its concrete items and systems of equipment and its human organization, skill and knowledge, springs from the stream of differences between sales proceeds of outputs and expenditures for inputs, which can be conceived to flow during future years from the firm's activities. It is indeed on this basis that 'the market' will seek to value these assets, or to value the 'going concern' which they compose. But there can be as many such valuations as there are different judges of the matter, each equipped with his own experience, training and temperament. The firm's belief in itself may be far different from the market's belief in it, and justifiably so. Again, even if some conjecture of the stream of trading revenues over future years were agreed, there is a second question: Does the market rate of interest provide the appropriate means of discounting future trading revenues to their value in today's spot cash? For if the firm makes successful use of the money which it has in hand today, that money may prove, in the end, to have grown at a much faster rate than would be represented by today's rate of interest. We can speak of the firm's 'internal rate of return', the percentage per annum at which its trading revenues over some stretch of years would have to be discounted to give a 'capitalized value' at the beginning of that stretch equal to the market's then valuation of the resources it commanded. A rate thus calculated from the *expected* trading revenues of a projected plant can serve to compare this plant with other schemes so as to judge which will pay best.

We shall argue that in studying the production plan, the search for complete logical rigour is self-defeating. The firm's practical and manageable problem is not to start with a clean slate and survey the entire range of technological and market possibilities, for using its abstract total value of resources, that the world presents. At any moment when policy or plan is being formed, the firm is a going concern engaged in a particular skein of activities, equipped with certain plant and staffed by men with certain skills and experience. The question to be answered (even if ruthlessly and without prejudices) is how to use these particular assets. And the assets may be divided into two kinds. There are, on one hand, those lands, forests, wells, buildings and machines which have been adapted for making products in a specific range. Regarding these the questions are: What particular variants of this range of products to produce, in what annual quantities, and by what methods? Whatever these outputs are to be, the firm will wish to manufacture them as cheaply as possible. One thing we shall therefore have to study (in Chapter 3) is the basic logic of cheapness in production. And whatever the nature of the products, the firm will wish to sell them to the best advantage. For this it must consider the formal connections between quantity and price, the logic of demand. The central concept here is that of price-elasticity, the question whether an x per cent reduction of price will elicit a greater or less than x per cent increase of quantities weekly or annually sold. This also is for Chapter 3.

The other kind of assets are the liquid ones: the money which the firm already has in the bank, the money which will flow from its activities of production and selling, and the money it can borrow from lenders or recruit from potential shareholders. This money can be used to make good the firm's equipment as it wears out, to replace it with up-to-date equipment as it becomes obsolete, to enlarge it for a greater flow of outputs, and to embark on entirely new ventures with newly discovered products made by newly invented technologies for newly created markets. *Investment*, in the economist's sense of the creation of physical, organizational and epistemic facilities for production, presents the firm with its most difficult occasions for decision. The plant and buildings it must order are extremely expensive. To repay this expense, they must be counted on to give service for years. Their success must thus depend on felicitous guessing of the circumstances of five or ten years hence. The vast powers bestowed by specialization are paid for by durability, and durability entails uncertainty.

Is there a logic of uncertainty? We shall claim that there is. But we shall distinguish this proposition absolutely from another with which it is very widely confused. A calculation requires two sorts of ingredient. There must be a logic of procedure, a method. And there must be data. It is very widely assumed that in confronting uncertainty, the possession of a method implies and carries with it the possession of objective data, observational measurements and facts. Uncertainty, however, means ignorance, and ignorance is the *absence* of facts. In especial, business success depends, in its most dramatic forms, on the exploitation of novelty, and novelty is that which has been *unknown* until now. We shall not labour this line of thought further until Chapter 4.

11. THE FIRM AND THE PUBLIC INTEREST

The firm has a purpose and forms policies in pursuit of it. But does this pursuit serve the interests of society at large? In *An Inquiry into the Causes of the Wealth of Nations* Adam Smith taught that it does. Systematic political economy sprang from a vision of economic society as an *organism*, where unconscious forces regulated themselves and each other in a system of inter-necessary activities, all dependent upon each and each dependent upon all. By producing what others want we make it their interest to produce what we want. Specialization and exchange make everyone immensely richer than isolated self-sufficiency could possibly do. By using as sparingly as possible the means available to him for production, and by choosing for each product those suitable means which are of least use in making other products, each man reduces the cost of his own product as part of his endeavour to maximize his own gain. But having minimized the *cost* of his own product, what compels him to sell it at a correspondingly low price? It is the fact that there are other sellers of this same product anxious to exchange it for what they need. *Competition* keeps prices keen. Competition is not a word with a single, simple meaning. But the bundle of related meanings that businessmen and economists give to it are extremely important in business management and economic analysis, and must have some attention as the concluding theme of this chapter.

The instinct of the philosopher is to search for simplicity and unifying coherence in his surroundings. A single principle of commanding simplicity which explains and embraces everything is perhaps his ideal. The economist, we may think, ought to have doubted the propriety of such a quest in his own field. For that field is superficial. It does not deal in the ultimate structure of things in the manner of the physicist and chemist, or of the biochemist or the geneticist, but with the most outward and complex aspect of the world, the end-product of all that Nature does in forming the human being and pouring in upon him a flood of conscious and unconscious impressions, building up memories and habits of thought of great intricacy, and throwing him into disturbing communication with thousands and millions of other human beings upon whom he must depend, and with whom he must contend, for the means of life. It may well be vain and illusory to seek for simplicity, unity and coherence in such a field. Yet the economist has some advantages in this respect over his fellow students of mankind. The market is a device expressly adapted to pre-reconcile human choices and co-ordinate human actions, and as a by-product of its fulfilment of this main task it provides a scale for reducing to one-dimensional 'wealth' the most heterogeneous collections of goods. Collaborative human action and a universal means of comparing the practical significance of goods are great achievements. They would be realized in the highest degree under so-called *perfect competition*.

Perfect competition assumes that every commodity can be defined and described in physical and technological terms, so that there is no doubt what we mean by 'soap', 'beer', or 'newsprint', at any rate when the grade is specified; and that each such commodity is produced by so many firms, of so even a size, that no one of them can appreciably affect the total output of all of them by any practicable change in its own output. When we stipulate that a commodity shall be technologically definable we mean to imply that two specimens of it which are technically and physically identical shall be accepted by every actual or potential purchaser as in every respect perfectly substitutable for each other, regardless of what firm produced one or the other of them, so that the purchaser does not mind which firm he buys from at a given price. Moreover, in the conditions we have stated, the price of every such specimen will in fact be uniform, provided that the market itself does its duty in instantly and universally diffusing knowledge of all transactions. For if any one firm tried to charge a higher price than others, it would lose all trade, while to charge a lower price is pointless, since it can sell at the market price all it can produce.

With the selling price of its commodity thus locked firmly into the impersonal control of the market, the firm has only to decide how much per unit of time to produce. At the higher of two market prices it can afford to increase output in face of difficulties that would have been too expensive at the lower price. Thus its most profitable output will be an increasing function of the market price. The same being true of every firm in the industry, the annual quantity of the commodity produced altogether can be represented, for given conditions outside the industry, by a curve which associates larger outputs with higher price and stays the same in shape and position. Such a *supply-curve* can only be drawn for an industry selling under perfect competition. Confronted with a demand-curve showing for each market price the annual quantity that would be bought, it seems able to determine for us the quantity that will annually be sold and the price per unit of these sales.

So long as an increment of output will cost less than the sale-proceeds of the result, the firm under perfect competition will wish to increase output. But in order to do so it will have to attract to itself, by the offer of suitable pay, means of production which might enable other firms and other industries profitably to expand their output. Thus if information is perfectly diffused in the markets for means of production, these means will go where they can earn most, and so eventually be so distributed over industries and firms, that there is no firm which can profitably employ any more of any of them, and no firm where they can earn higher pay than the one they are in. Even when it cannot profitably increase its output, a firm may be selling its existing output as a whole for more than that output costs in means of production. But if so, there will be businessmen (so the argument runs) ready to set up new firms to share in that profitable trade. Their additions to the market supply will bring down the market price to the level where every firm which survives in the industry is just and only just covering the unavoidable costs of the output it is producing. When this is true in all industries throughout the society, it will be possible to claim that the means of production are optimally allocated over the various lines of production, and that in the entire productive picture, those things are being produced in those quantities which, given their prices which are equal to their costs, are desired by the members of the society. Perfect competition, in sum, when we assume it to prevail in all markets both for products and means of production, and if we assume a fair distribution of ownership of these means, shows us a universal and simple principle which, acting through price, *allocates* means of production to the best general advantage.

In the vastly different real conditions of the last third of the twentieth century, firms are still the instruments of allocation of more than half of the British society's resources. But they are not content that this allocation shall merely reflect the natural and spontaneous tastes of the society. Hundreds of millions of pounds are annually spent in suggesting to it new tastes and in inventing new things for it to want, and in fostering a mutual emulation of its members in ostentatious consumption. It may be reasonable to ask whether the theory of the firm might not concern itself with the ethics and social effects of the firm's activities and not merely with their efficiency in making profits. Here we shall not undertake that task. But there is a question which we cannot avoid. The ascendancy which was exercised for decades and even for centuries by the notion of more or less effective competition has been due, as we have shown, to two considerations. One was the belief in its practical power of optimizing the use of resources. The other was its intellectual advantage of seeming to offer a universal and simple account of the sources and effects of all economic conduct. If the basis of that theory has vanished, can we replace it by a different theory without stultifying our own efforts by the complexity to which we may be driven?

CHAPTER 2

The Matrix of Production

The business of production as a whole which is going on in a society at any moment can be dissected in countless ways into distinct partial activities and into sectors where these contributory processes take place. A scheme of analysis which is meant to suggest or guide action should conform in some way to the existing division of production amongst decision-making centres; that is to say, amongst firms or such groups of firms as make broadly similar products. Every such firm or industry stands at the confluence of many streams of products which it buys from other sectors, and itself supplies its product directly to many other sectors and through them to the whole productive organism. Each sector also supplies its product direct to final users, comprising consumers who will use the goods for enjoyment and sustenance, businessmen investing in durable equipment which will not itself be passed on to other firms, and the government. The output of each sector (measured by the value of goods sold and not merely by the value which has been added in the sector) thus goes partly for *intermediate use* and partly for *final use*. The involvement of almost all sectors in supplying each other directly and indirectly with means of further production implies that the total quantity annually required of any product, for final and intermediate uses taken together, depends on the respective *final use quantities* required of *all products*. To find and express this dependence in quantitative terms by a system of equations is the purpose of *input–output analysis*. Activity, product and sector are classes so conceived in input–output analysis that they stand in one-to-one correspondence with each other. Each activity is deemed to result in only one product, each product to be made by only one activity. Each activity is carried on in only one sector and each sector has only one activity. To allow every technological, geographical or market distinction to define a separate product would result in a list of millions of products. Practical computation can handle only a few hundreds. Each *product* in input–output analysis is therefore a bundle of commodities made up to be as meaningful as available statistics and the needs of computation allow. For the reason that products are composite if for no other, direct physical measurement

34

of commodities is inappropriate, and quantity of product will be represented by value at given prices.

In the exchange of products amongst sectors, each sector is both a producer of one product and a purchaser of others. When we have divided the totality of production into n sectors, we shall label these sectors $1, 2, \ldots, n$. When we wish to refer to the representative producing sector we shall call it sector i. For the representative purchasing sector we shall speak of sector j. The product of sector i will be called product i. The value at given prices of what is annually bought by sector j from sector i will be written X_{ij}, and when this is divided by the value Z_j of what is annually sold to both final and intermediate users taken together by sector j, we shall call the quotient an input coefficient and write it a_{ij}:

$$a_{ij} = X_{ij}/Z_{ij}$$

Thus $a_{2,5}$ will stand for the quantity (measured in value at given prices) of product 2 required for making *one unit* of product 5. Each Z_i, the total quantity annually demanded of product i for both intermediate and final use taken together (that is, for *total use*) will consist of all the quantities $a_{ij}Z_j$ required by producers for their productive purposes, together with the quantity Y_i demanded by final users. Or given the total quantity Z_i annually available of product i, we can subtract from this the quantity $\sum_{j=1}^{n} a_{ij}Z_j$ required by producers and find the quantity Y_i available for final users:

$$Z_i - \sum_{j=1}^{n} a_{ij}Z_j = Y_i \qquad (2.1)$$

where the summation symbol $\sum_{j=1}^{n}$ gives instructions to make stand successively for every number from 1 up to n, both inclusive, and then to add together all the resulting terms $a_{ij}Z_j$. Equation (2.1) expresses the dependence of the quantity Y_i of product i, annually available for final use, on the total quantity Z_i annually produced of product i and on the quantity of product i annually required for intermediate use. This intermediate use requirement of product i depends in turn on the respective total quantities produced of all the n products. Thus equation (2.1) shows Y_i as a function of all the Z_j, including Z_i itself. An equation like (2.1) can evidently be written for each of the n products. The information given by these equations is, however, 'the wrong way round' for our purpose. What we desire is to express the dependence of the *total* annual requirement of *each* product on each and every one of the n respective annual quantities Y_i demanded for *final use*. That is to say, we seek a set of equations in each of which, not Y_i, but Z_i, will stand by itself on one side of the 'equals' sign, and the manner in which this Z_i is determined will be exhibited on the other side of the 'equals' sign in an expression containing the final use quantity of every one of the products. To get this second form of statement out of the other form, to turn the first kind of equations round, is to *solve* these equations. The entire sequence of steps, leading from the raw data of annual quantities sold of each product for its various applications, to the solution which enables the respective required total outputs to be calculated from any arbitrarily chosen or given 'bill of goods for final use', is best expressed and carried through in *matrix notation*.

Let us consider a productive system consisting of three sectors, and write W_i for the annual quantity required of product i for intermediate use. Then the three intermediate-use quantities can be expressed as three equations, which it will be tidy and convenient to write one below another:

$$\left.\begin{aligned} a_{11}Z_1 + a_{12}Z_2 + a_{13}Z_3 &= W_1 \\ a_{21}Z_1 + a_{22}Z_2 + a_{23}Z_3 &= W_2 \\ a_{31}Z_1 + a_{32}Z_2 + a_{33}Z_3 &= W_3 \end{aligned}\right\} \qquad (2.2)$$

Because, in general, each of the n products of a complete productive system is required as an input in the making of *each* of these n products, we require altogether $n \times n$ input coefficients a_{ij} to express the quantitative pattern of production, so that in our 3-product system, above, we have 3×3 such coefficients. The number of such coefficients is necessarily a perfect square, and this is well suggested if we write the coefficients in a table by themselves exactly as they occur in the above three equations. The result is a 3×3 *square matrix:*

$$\begin{bmatrix} a_{11} & a_{12} & a_{13} \\ a_{21} & a_{22} & a_{23} \\ a_{31} & a_{32} & a_{33} \end{bmatrix}$$

Now, to indicate that each of these coefficients is to be multiplied by the appropriate Z_j, we write the three Z_j in a 3×1 matrix or *column vector* at the right-hand side:

$$\begin{bmatrix} a_{11} & a_{12} & a_{13} \\ a_{21} & a_{22} & a_{23} \\ a_{31} & a_{32} & a_{33} \end{bmatrix} \begin{bmatrix} Z_1 \\ Z_2 \\ Z_3 \end{bmatrix}$$

The convention for multiplying together two matrices arises simply and directly from its use as a way of writing a system of equations such as (2.2). Let us start with the first row of a's. All of these a's

36

have their first subscript in common, namely a 1 showing that they stand in the first row. The second subscript of each a shows its column. It is these column-subscripts which are to be matched with the row-subscripts of the Z's. Thus a_{11} is paired with Z_1, a_{12} is paired with Z_2, and a_{13} is paired with Z_3. The two factors composing each pair are multiplied together, giving us $a_{11}Z_1$, $a_{12}Z_2$, and $a_{13}Z_3$. These three products of multiplication are then added together, and we have the left-hand side of the first equation of (2.2). Moving to the second row of a's, we match their column-subscripts with the row-subscripts of the Z's, multiply and add as before, and thus we have the left-hand side of the second equation of (2.2). And similarly with the third row of a's and the third equation. Before proceeding, we may notice here the rule which results from this convention. Two matrices, one standing on the left of the other, can be multiplied together if, and only if, the left-hand one has as many elements (entries) in each row as the right-hand one has elements in each column. Thus an $m \times n$ matrix can be multiplied by an $n \times p$ matrix standing on its right, and the result will be an $m \times p$ matrix. Two matrices, which we may simply call A and Z, can in some cases be multiplied together when A stands on the left and Z on the right, but not when their positions are changed round. In our illustration, indeed, we can form the product AZ but not the product ZA. In cases where both products can be formed, as will be the case when A has enough columns to match Z's rows, and Z has enough columns to match A's rows, the products of AZ and ZA will in general be different from each other. Matrix multiplication is *non-commutative*. By this procedure of matrix multiplication, we can write the equation-system (2.2) in matrix form as

$$AZ = W \tag{2.3}$$

Let us now write out, for our three-sector system, the set of equations we have to solve. We have already seen the type of one such equation in Σ notation:

$$Z_i - \sum_{j=1}^{n} a_{ij} Z_j = Y_i \tag{2.1}$$

We shall now need three such equations, which we will write out in full:

$$\left.\begin{array}{l} Z_1 - (a_{11}Z_1 + a_{12}Z_2 + a_{13}Z_3) = Y_1 \\ Z_2 - (a_{21}Z_1 + a_{22}Z_2 + a_{23}Z_3) = Y_2 \\ Z_3 - (a_{31}Z_1 + a_{32}Z_2 + a_{33}Z_3) = Y_3 \end{array}\right\} \tag{2.4}$$

We have seen above how to write the 3×3 terms in brackets, as one whole, in matrix form, viz. $W = AZ$. The column of Z's, from which the bracket terms have to be subtracted, can be treated as a 3×1

37

matrix or column vector and simply written Z, and the column of Y's, as one whole, can be simply written Y. Thus the whole system of three equations can be written.

$$Z - AZ = Y \qquad (2.5)$$

and it is this matrix equation that we wish to solve.

When, in ordinary algebra, we wish to turn the equation $ax = y$, which expresses the value of y in terms of a and x, into one which expresses the value of x in terms of a and y, we first write down the reciprocal of a, that is, the symbol which, when multiplied by a in the ordinary arithmetical way, will give us unity: $a \times (1/a) = 1$. Then multiplying both sides of the equation by this reciprocal we have $x = (1/a)y$, and this is the *solution*. In matrix algebra, as in ordinary algebra, we have a symbol which *leaves unchanged* anything which is multiplied by it. In ordinary algebra this is *one*, or *unity*. In matrix algebra it is the *identity matrix*. This is a square matrix of any required number of rows and the same number of columns, having one (unity) everywhere in the *main diagonal* running from top left to bottom right-hand corner and zeros elsewhere. The 3×3 identity is accordingly

$$I_3 = \begin{bmatrix} 1 & 0 & 0 \\ 0 & 1 & 0 \\ 0 & 0 & 1 \end{bmatrix}$$

since

$$\begin{bmatrix} 1 & 0 & 0 \\ 0 & 1 & 0 \\ 0 & 0 & 1 \end{bmatrix} \begin{bmatrix} Z_1 \\ Z_2 \\ Z_3 \end{bmatrix} = \begin{bmatrix} Z_1 \\ Z_2 \\ Z_3 \end{bmatrix}$$

and this enables us to slightly simplify our equation by writing $(I - A)Z$ instead of $Z - AZ$. Thus it becomes

$$(I - A)Z = Y \qquad (2.6)$$

where $(I - A)$ is called the Leontief matrix after the inventor of input–output analysis. If it were possible to find a matrix $(I - A)^{-1}$, the *inverse* of $(I - A)$, such that when $(I - A)$ is multiplied by it the product is the identity matrix, then we could multiply both sides of equation (2.6) by $(I - A)^{-1}$ and thus solve it:

$$(I - A)^{-1}(I - A)Z = (I - A)^{-1}Y$$

or

$$IZ = (I - A)^{-1}Y$$

or

$$Z = (I - A)^{-1}Y$$

or for short

$$Z = RY$$

THE MATRIX OF PRODUCTION

A square matrix (such as the Leontief matrix) has an inverse provided that its rows are *linearly independent*, that is to say, provided we cannot reproduce any one of these rows by multiplying some other rows respectively by numbers λ_i and adding together the resulting new rows. Provided the rows of an $n \times n$ matrix A are linearly independent, A^{-1} (read 'A inverse') is built up one column at a time by solving n systems of linear equations each of the form $A s_{ij} = e_i$, where s_{ij} is the jth column of the inverse and e_i is a column-vector whose i^{th} element (i^{th} row) is 1 and whose other elements are all zero. If A is a 3×3 matrix we should have, for example,

$$\begin{bmatrix} a_{11} & a_{12} & a_{13} \\ a_{21} & a_{22} & a_{23} \\ a_{31} & a_{32} & a_{33} \end{bmatrix} \begin{bmatrix} s_1 \\ s_2 \\ s_3 \end{bmatrix} = \begin{bmatrix} 1 \\ 0 \\ 0 \end{bmatrix}$$

as the system to be solved in order to obtain the first column, s_{i1}, of the inverse. The second column of the inverse would be the solution of a like system having as its right-hand side

$$e_2 = \begin{bmatrix} 0 \\ 1 \\ 0 \end{bmatrix}$$

and so on.

A system of n linear equations in n unknowns can be solved by a process of elimination and substitution. Indeed, the system (2.4) above could be solved direct in that manner. But the solution so found would be a solution of that particular system only, having on its right-hand side the particular column of Y_i. By finding an inverse for the matrix of input coefficients, A, we obtain a general solution which can be used to find the column of total outputs Z_j required for *any* given 'bill of quantities for final use' Y. We may note in conclusion that, though matrix multiplication is in general non-commutative, the multiplication of a square matrix by its inverse is commutative, and we have by definition $A A^{-1} = A^{-1} A = I$.

CHAPTER 3

The Firm's Tests of Rightness

1. VARIABLES, VALUES, VECTORS AND FUNCTIONS

In order to choose its action in some respect, at some moment, the firm needs a clearly formulated purpose which the action is to subserve; a knowledge of the circumstances with which the action has to deal; and a test to determine whether any proposed action is the best. The purpose we have ascribed to the firm, by way of definition of the concept of a firm, is that of making as large as it can the excess of the value of its planned outputs over that of its planned inputs, when each of the payments actually to be made or received for these, if treated as known for certain, is discounted at the market rate of interest from its own future date to the date of making the plan. In Chapter 1 we distinguished durable tools on one hand from materials and services on the other, and we distinguished the long period, in which even the most durable tools and facilities, and those taking the longest time to construct, are the result of today's planning, from the short period, in which some of the facilities are inherited from the past, cannot be quickly altered, and are included amongst those circumstances which the plan has to take as given and fixed for the time being. The short period gives us two advantages when we wish to examine the logic of choice step by step from the simplest cases. It absolves us from considering *investment*, the acquisition of durable tools whose worthwhileness depends on a present reckoning of the services they will render over a long stretch of future years in a variety of supposable conditions; and it enables us without gross absurdity to assume that the firm has full knowledge of the effects of each of the rival actions open to it. In this chapter we shall illustrate some general logical principles of choice by considering the firm's short-period production problems on the supposition that it possesses all relevant technical and market knowledge. Subsequent chapters will show that these principles still play a part even when the firm's policy problem is transformed in its foundations by the recognition of potential novelty and invention, and by the uncertainty which these engender. First, however, we shall seek to by-pass the mathematicians without offending them, by suggesting how some

40

required mathematical notions can be seen to arise in natural succession from the practical idea of measurement.

If, at nine o'clock each morning, we measure the height of a seedling to which we have given an identity by sticking a label in the ground beside it, the resulting series of measurements will have in some respects a common origin. They will all be measurements of one and the same characteristic of one and the same object, though made on different dates. It will be reasonable to call them a class of measurements. Such measurements could still be called a class if they were the heights of a collection of seedlings at some one moment. To qualify as a class, the measurements ought, we may feel, to have something in common with each other, as to the characteristic in question or the objects possessing it or some other circumstance. Let us further extend the idea of a class of measurements by including, besides measurements which have actually been made in specific circumstances, all those which might be made in the same circumstances. We shall call a class of actual or conceivable measurements a variable quantity or simply a *variable*. Thus we have two notions to begin with:

a *measurable* is a set of circumstances of measurement;
a *variable* is a class of measurements, actual or conceivable, made in some specified invariant set of circumstances.

Measurement consists in comparison of the objects to be measured with a standard object, called, in respect of the characteristic in question, a unit. Measurement is expressed as a *number* of units. The *range* of a variable is all those numbers which can appear as members of the particular class of measurements. The range may be, for example, all the natural numbers $1, 2, 3, \ldots$, or all the whole numbers positive and negative together with zero, or all the real numbers including all rationals and irrationals. The range of a variable is a set of symbols or numbers to which the member-measurements of the class of measurements are confined, if they are to belong to the variable. What is variable about a class of measurements is not, of course, the class as a whole, which depends for its identity on conforming to a given specification of its circumstances. What is variable is the particular member of the class which we happen to have selected for momentary attention. A collection of paintings in a gallery may not change, but the answer to the question 'Which painting are you looking at?' does change. Each particular *number* of units constituting a member of some class of measurements is a *value* of the variable in question. Thus we have a third notion:

a *value* of a variable is a particular member of the class of numbers constituting that variable.

41

Many variables can evidently be considered together, and we can select one value from each variable in our list and regard the resulting set of values as an entity in itself, a single and unified whole. Such a list of specified values, one from each of a specified list of variables, is a *vector:*

> a vector contains one value from each of a stated list of variables. No manipulation is performed on the values in order that they may compose a vector. A vector consists in the *association* of these values and their treatment as forming a single whole.

Vectors themselves can compose a class. A principle or rule, no matter how specified, for selecting from amongst the vectors which can be formed from a given list of variables, certain vectors and excluding all others, is a function. It may be compared to the rule for membership of a club, which may confine the club, for example, to persons over sixty years old. The function will specify some quantitative relations which must subsist amongst the values which compose any given vector, if it is to qualify for membership of the class of vectors in question. Thus, for example, it may stipulate that each of two variables shall range over the real number continuum, and that in each vector composing the function, one value, called y, shall be the square of the other, called x: $y = x^2$. In this *notation*, x is a generic name for all members of one variable, and can represent any value of that variable. Similarly of course y is a name for every member of the other variable.

Notations for representing values, variables, vectors and functions are chiefly two. There is the algebraic notation where letters from the end of the alphabet stand for variables, and letters from the beginning of the alphabet stand for individual numbers which we are treating as given and constant for the argument in hand without wishing, or perhaps being able, to say what these numbers are. Secondly there is the brilliant spatial analog of algebra, called Cartesian geometry, which treats all quantities as lengths and measures the lengths representing values of two different variables as distances along, or parallel to, two straight lines at right angles to each other, using each of these straight lines or *axes* as the starting line for measurements along, or parallel to, the other *axis*. If we have three variables we need, of course, three axes at right angles to each other, and with still more variables the visual scheme fails us, though not its principle. A vector associates with each other two (or more) particular values, each from a different variable. Thus in the Cartesian scheme it associates with each other two particular distances each measured from one or other axis to a line parallel to that axis. Where these lines intersect at right-angles there is a *point* whose distances from the axes represent the particular values of the variables. This *point* thus represents in itself the association of the two values, and is the geometrical representation of what in algebra we have spoken of as a *vector*.

Once we have drawn our Cartesian axes at right angles and selected a unit of length for measuring distances *from* one axis and *parallel* to the other, we have a scheme where every vector has its one and only one corresponding point which represents and specifies it, and where every point has its one and only one vector or ordered pair of numbers which specifies and locates the point. Cartesian points and algebraic vectors are merely two names for the same idea. If, then, a function is a rule for selecting some vectors out of all those which could be formed from the two variables in question (whatever these variables may be in terms of the nature of their *measurables*), it is plain that a function is a rule for selecting some *points* and excluding all the others. The nature of this rule of selection will be some quantitative relation betweeen the respective values which compose an admissible vector. Thus in our example above, any vector belongs to the function provided its y-value is the square of its x-value. The different forms which functions can take are, in the strictest sense, not merely beyond counting (that is, beyond being placed in one-to-one correspondence with the infinity of natural numbers) but beyond the cardinality of even the real number continuum, which includes the fractions and the irrationals. Yet it is the relatively simple forms, having an intuitively apprehendable character, that are useful to the scientist and the economist. Indeed, for the economist, the simplest form of all, the linear relation exemplified by $y = ax + b$ is the most useful of all, and even the compound interest function, $y = a^x$, whatever potentialities it may wrap up, is a perfect illustration of the idea that functions are architecture, they are *structure with a purpose*.

Every feature which can be found in the algebraic statement of a function appears also, of course, in its geometric picture. Suppose the selection rule for vectors or points of the function is that in each vector the value of y shall be 5 less twice the value of x, or $y = 5 - 2x$. In order to graph the function we shall assign a succession of numerical values to x, work out for each of these values its corresponding value of y, and plot a point at the appropriate pair of distances from the axes of the Cartesian diagram:

for x equal to	0	1	2	3	4...
y has the value	5	3	1	-1	$-3...$

Negative values of x will be measured to the left of the point of intersection of the axes, positive values to the right of it; negative values of y will be measured downwards from the x-axis, positive values upwards from it. The points given above will appear as in Fig. 3.1.

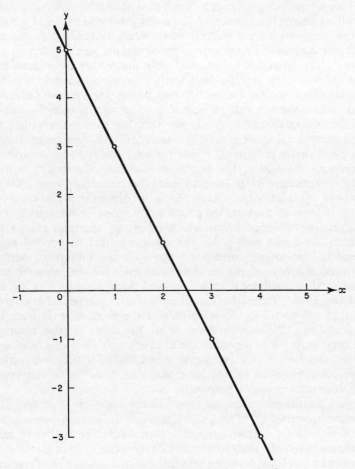

The curve (a straight line) of $y = 5 - 2x$.

FIG. 3.1.

Several things in this picture leap to the eye. All the points lie on a straight line, and it is natural to assume that other points of the function also lie on this line, so that we can justifiably draw a continuous segment of this line through the plotted points and beyond

44

them. Our function is for this reason called *linear*. Next, the line slopes down from left to right. That is to say, larger values of x are associated with smaller values of y. And when we study the relative size of the differences between any pair of values of x, and the corresponding pair of values of y, we find that their ratio is everywhere the same. This is a feature of a straight line, or linear, function, and of no other function.

In reckoning a difference between two values of x, it will be natural to subtract the smaller from the larger. But when we wish to find the *corresponding* difference between values of y, we must use, as the value to be taken away, that value of y which corresponds to the smaller of the two values of x. In our example, this means that a larger will be taken from a smaller value of y, and the resulting difference will be negative, a *minus quantity*. This *minus* appears in our equation for the function. It is the minus of the coefficient of x, the minus sign of the 2 by which x is to be multiplied in $y = 5 - 2x$. Lastly, when in this equation we put $x = 0$, we are bound to get a point lying on the y-axis; for putting $x = 0$ means that the distance of the corresponding point from the y-axis is zero. And when we put $y = 0$ we shall for the same reason get a point on the x-axis. These two points are the intercepts of the line $y = 5 - 2x$ on the y-axis and the x-axis respectively.

In describing the plotting of points for Fig. 3.1 we spoke of finding for each value of x its corresponding value of y. The function idea, when two variables only are involved, is essentially that of a pairing or partnering of values, one from each variable, so as to establish a pattern in which one and only one value of y corresponds to, or is associated with, each value of x and one and only one value of x corresponds to each value of y. Such a pattern is called a one-to-one correspondence. More strictly, we ought to speak of such a function as monotonically increasing or monotonically decreasing, since many algebraic expressions of a function rule will assign a given value of y to more than one value of x. The essence of the function idea is the association of particular values, related to each other in a way common to all vectors of the function. When a function is written with one of the variables standing alone on one side of the 'equals' sign and the rest of the symbols on the other side, we can speak of the solitary symbol as the dependent variable and the other variable as the independent variable. The roles of the two variables can be interchanged by solving the equation. Thus from $y = 5 - 2x$ we get $x = (5 - y)/2$. 'Dependent' and 'independent' refer to the formal role of a variable in the momentary form which an equation has been given. It has no necessary connection with any idea of 'cause and effect'.

2. DIFFERENCE-QUOTIENT, DERIVATIVE, DIFFERENTIATION

The idea of comparing the mutually corresponding differences of two variables that are associated in a function is a most vital one for economists. When, as in Fig. 3.1, the *curve* representing the function is a straight line, the ratio of corresponding differences (the difference-quotient) is everywhere the same. But when the curve representing a function is a curve also in the conversational sense, its ratio of differences will vary from one part of the curve to another. Moreover it will vary according as we take large or small differences for comparison. How can the comparison of differences be standardized, as it were, so that this latter effect does not confuse the issue? We can do so by comparing the differences, not of the curve itself, but of the straight line which touches the curve, without crossing it, at that point of the curve which we are for the moment interested in. The difference-quotient read off from this *tangent* is the *slope* of the curve at the point of tangency. This slope varies, of course, as we proceed along the curve, and if the curve expresses a function-rule associating the two variables, there will be, implicit in the situation, another function-rule associating the slope of the curve with the value of the independent variable. This other function, derived from the first one, is called the (first) *derivative*.

The notion of the derivative is the basis of the classical mathematical method of finding that value of one variable to which there corresponds a locally greatest or least value of the other, a *maximum* or a *minimum*. Suppose that as we move through a succession of increasing values of one variable, the corresponding values of the other variable first rise and then fall. At some value of the first variable, the second variable will be at a value greater than it takes at neighbouring points, it will have a maximum. Or if, as we proceed to successively greater values of the first variable, the second assumes first successively smaller and then successively larger values, then there will be a value of the first variable to which there will correspond a minimum of the second. It will be characteristic of those points where the second variable is at a maximum, or at a minimum, that a small difference of the first variable will make no difference to the second variable, for that second variable has, as it were, ceased increasing but not yet begun to decline, or has ceased declining but not yet begun to rise. At the top of the hill, or at the bottom of the valley, we walk for the moment on the level. If, therefore, we had a method of determining that value of the first variable, where a small increment or decrement of this value makes no difference, a zero difference, to the second variable, we should have a method of locating the maximum or minimum of the second variable.

Differentiation can be thought of as selecting, from a collection of standard formulae, the one appropriate to any particular type of function, and applying it, perhaps in combination with other such formulae, to obtain the algebraic expression of the derivative of that function. The derivative is itself a function. If the function whose derivative we require expresses y as depending on x, then the derivative of y with respect to x, written dy/dx (dy by dx) will also in general depend on x, that is to say, if dy/dx stands by itself on the left-hand side of an equation, the right-hand side will be an expression involving x. Such formulae for the derivative can of course be proved. But in practice the user of the differential calculus knows them by heart or looks them up. Frequently needed examples are $dx^n = nx^{n-1}$ where n is an integer greater than zero, and $de^{kx}/dx = ke^{kx}$ when k is a real number. That is our justification for describing differentiation as a mere formula-selecting process.

Once we have an expression for the derivative, any maximum or minimum of the original function can begin to be tracked down by setting this derivative equal to zero, and seeking to solve the resulting equation to find a numerical value for the independent variable. That value will be the one which, in case of a hump-shaped function or segment of curve, gives the function its locally greatest value, or if the curve sags in a loop, gives the locally least value. We shall merely illustrate the matter, in a simple case, without proof.

The curve $y = -\tfrac{1}{2}x^2 + 2x + 5$ can be plotted as far as necessary from the following table and is shown in Fig. 3.2

$x =$	-2	-1	0	1	2	3	4	5	6
$y =$	-1	$5/2$	5	$13/2$	7	$13/2$	5	$5/2$	-1

Here the top of the hill can be easily seen to be at a point $x = 2$, $y = 7$ To locate it analytically we differentiate the expression for y as a function of x:

$$dy/dx = -x + 2$$

and set this derivative equal to zero:

$$-x + 2 = 0$$
$$x = 2$$

If, in the expression $dy/dx = -x + 2$, we give x a smaller value than 2, the derivative will have a greater-than-zero numerical value; it will be positive. At such values of x, therefore, the difference of y corresponding to a positive difference of x must itself be positive, that is to say, as x increases, y will increase also, and the curve $y = y(x)$ will slope upwards from left to right. (Here we have written

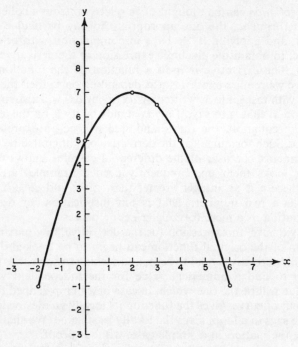

FIG. 3.2.

$$y = -\tfrac{1}{2}x^2 + 2x + 5 \quad dy/dx = -x + 2 = 0$$
$$x = 2$$

y is a function of x in the accepted shorthand notation without specifying the character of *y*'s dependence on *x*.) At values of *x* greater than the one which makes *y* a maximum, *dy/dx* will be negative and the curve will slope downwards to the right. We claimed, above, that every feature of the function is expressed in both its algebraic and its geometrical representation. In the graph of the function, a visible feature of the upward-sloping segment is that the slope gets less and less steep as we move to greater values of *x*. The downward-sloping segment gets more and more steep. But algebraically speaking, these two phenomena are the same. Numerically increasing negative values are treated as algebraically decreasing values. Thus throughout the segment of the curve shown in Fig. 3.2, the *slope of the curve decreases algebraically*. This fact must appear in the equation of the curve, and it does appear when we differentiate the expression for the (first) derivative to get the second derivative:

$$\frac{d}{dx}\left(\frac{dy}{dx}\right) = -1 \quad \text{or} \quad \frac{d^2x}{dx^2} = -1$$

In the particular case of the function $y = -\frac{1}{2}x^2 + 2x + 5$ (and in the case of all such quadratic expressions) the second derivative is a constant. In our case it is negative, and this shows that as x increases, the slope of the curve $y = y(x)$ decreases. In fact, the negative second derivative shows that $y = -\frac{1}{2}x^2 + 2x + 5$ is the expression of a hill and not a valley, and thus indicates that the extreme value found by putting the derivative equal to zero is a hill-top or maximum and not a valley-bottom or minimum.

3. THREE DIMENSIONS REPRESENTED IN TWO DIMENSIONS

So much for functions which associate together values of two variables. Functions which associate three variables require for their geometry a space of three dimensions, that is, three directions of measurement each at right-angles to each of the others. If two straight lines intersecting at right-angles on a table-top indicate two of these directions, a third will be shown by a wire stuck vertically into the table at their intersection, that is, at the *origin* of the system of co-ordinate axes. A function which involves only two variables, say x and $y(x)$, is pictured geometrically by a curve on a flat plane. A function which associates three variables requires a *surface*. Not merely the profile of a hill-side, but the hill itself 'in the round' can now be represented. A point on the hill-side will be located by three distances; for example, its distance eastwards from one base-line, its distance northwards from a second base-line, and its altitude above sea level. In abstract terms, it will be a vector of three elements or components: (x, y, z). The selective principle of the function will still consist in stipulated relations amongst the permitted values of these variables. The forms which such functions can take are again, of course, numerous beyond counting, and beyond even the next greater infinity after that of the integers. The economist, however, is likely to be concerned with relatively simple forms, and even at that, with types or classes of such forms rather than specific forms. He may be interested, for example, in a type of 'hill-side' whose slope is constant, provided one walks along a straight path from the origin, but is not constant if one sets off from some other point than the origin and walks parallel to one of the axes. This particular type of 'hill-side' throws light on problems of production when we use the two base-plane axes to represent quantities of productive services, and the vertical axis to represent quantity of product per time unit, that is, *output*. *Production functions* of this and other types will

D 49

concern us below. But how are they to be pictured on the flat page of a book?

The ingenious answer was invented by map makers centuries ago, indeed a map is a two-dimensional representation of a three-dimensional vector. Points on the earth's surface are in a three-space (if you like, latitude, longitude and altitude), but the page of the atlas shows only a two-space of latitude and longitude. For altitude it resorts to contour lines. In economics, the versatility and applications of the same formal device are endless.

A contour line is a function associating two variables only. For the geographer these are latitude and longitude, for the economist they can be weekly or yearly quantities used up of means of production or of consumable goods, or quantities of assets of different kinds possessed, and so on. In any such function, the selective principle is the requirement that only those points or paired quantities (x, y) are included in the contour line, which according to some specific function in the three-space, are all associated with one and the same value of the third variable z. If the three-variable function is a 'hill-side', the contour lines are revealed by slicing it horizontally, parallel to the base-plane or xy-plane. But we can also slice it vertically, at right-angles to the xy-plane and parallel to one of the base-plane axes. A section parallel to the x-axis will show us a profile of the hill which will again represent a two-dimensional function, one which involves in this case only x and z. Such a profile will have a varying steepness of slope which we can write dz/dx. It is a most convenient fact that if the surface or 'hill-side' in question is continuous in a particular, precise mathematical sense, we can treat the steepness of slope of the hill in *any* direction as a 'weighted sum' of its steepness parallel to the x-axis and its steepness parallel to the y-axis. Thus if we follow a path which carries us a short distance Δx in the x-direction at the same time as it carries us a short distance Δy (in general, of different size from Δx) in the y-direction, the distance we shall thus climb in the z-direction will be

$$\Delta z = \frac{\partial z}{\partial x} \Delta x + \frac{\partial z}{\partial y} \Delta y$$

The symbol ∂ (dabba) is here used instead of d to indicate a partial derivative, that is, the derivative of a function with respect to one out of the several variables on which it depends. Now if we were to follow some one contour line we should, by definition, not climb (or descend) at all. So we should have

$$\Delta z = \frac{\partial z}{\partial x} \Delta x + \frac{\partial z}{\partial y} \Delta y = 0$$

50

and thus (dividing both sides of the equation by Δx)

$$\frac{\partial z}{\partial x} + \frac{\partial z}{\partial y}\frac{\Delta y}{\Delta x} = 0$$

In the limit as Δx tends to zero $\Delta y/\Delta x$ tends to dy/dx, so that

$$\frac{\partial z}{\partial x} + \frac{\partial z}{\partial y}\frac{dy}{dx} = 0$$

or

$$\frac{dy}{dx} = -\frac{\partial z}{\partial x}\bigg/\frac{\partial z}{\partial y}$$

When the contour line, $y = y(x)$, is thought of purely as connecting with each other values of y and x, its slope in the y-direction will be related, as shown in the foregoing expression, to the shape of the hill-side of which this contour line is a section.

4. THE LOGIC OF CHEAPNESS

Economics has traditionally tended to concern itself with problems of proportions. Each means of production and each product was viewed as something given in quality and character by Nature. Men's choice was limited to combining them in various relative quantities. A man could choose how to divide his time between work and leisure, or his income between bread, beer and coal. A farmer could use more land or more labour but their technical employments made up a fixed art. With Alfred Marshall in late Victorian times, this view was already dissolving, but it has left its mark on the character of economics as a scholarly subject. Economists expressly repudiate any concern with problems of engineering, biology or the origin of human tastes and psychic constitution. These disciplines provide him with given facts which it is not his purpose to improve on. Gerald Shove rejected the implications of this view in relation to production and saw each man, machine and acre of land as something as individual as a piece of a jigsaw puzzle, and the firm's chief problem as the careful fitting together of these pieces. *How much?* is the typical question asked by economists, and it obscures many issues and elides many difficulties which remain hidden to upset their conclusions. How much ought a firm to spend on research? The question is basically unanswerable, since the new knowledge which is the goal of research cannot be evaluated until it has been discovered. We do not know what it will cost to answer particular questions, we do not know what a given line of research will uncover. At a less philosophical level, we may claim that the question 'How?' is as essential as the question 'How much?'. Recent experience in aircraft policy has shown what huge sums can be spent to no useful effect. But in this chapter we are concerned with classic lines of thought. On these lines, the questions for a firm already established in some industry are: By what combination of factors of production to produce any particular output (quantity per time-unit) of its product which it might choose? And given the cheapest method of producing each output, what output to choose?

By *factor of production* early economists meant such a category as human services or the capacities of the basic natural environment. So long as production was deemed to be purely agricultural, and of stable composition, the diversity within the category of 'labour' or 'land' did not prevent meaningful rough measurement. But a factor of production must for us be composed of specimens identical in all those respects which are relevant to their productive performance. There will thus, of course, be millions rather than thousands of different factors and the shortcomings of the purely quantitative treatment of production policy are thus exposed. Nonetheless we can illustrate the basic logic of cheapness by supposing that some product requires only two factors of production, each quite homogeneous. A quantity of factor x which the firm might employ will be represented by a distance measured on the west–east axis and a quantity of factor y by a distance on the north–south axis. Let us picture these two axes by two adjacent edges of a table-top. Any point on the table-top will thus represent some pair of quantities of the two factors. Output, the weekly quantity of product, will be represented by distances z measured vertically upwards from the table-top parallel to an axis of altitude for which we can suppose a straight wire to be stuck into the table top at the corner where the west–east and north–south axes meet. By means of the three coordinate axes thus provided, we can represent any vector of three numbers (x,y,z), such as the output z corresponding to any pair of factor-quantities (x,y), by a point in the air above the table-top, and we can represent any continuous function associating these three variables with each other by a surface, such as the hill of production we have already spoken of. In Fig. 3.3 we have sought for the sake of immediacy of comprehension to suggest this hill of production by means of a perspective drawing. Here the two factor-axes, because of this perspective, appear at an acute angle instead of a right-angle as they really are. In order to convey the rounded solidity of the hill we have shown its sides as rising abruptly from the xy-plane, whereas it might more plausibly be shown as having some greater-than-zero altitude at every point of the north-east quadrant. In this picture also we have shown a few specimens of the contour

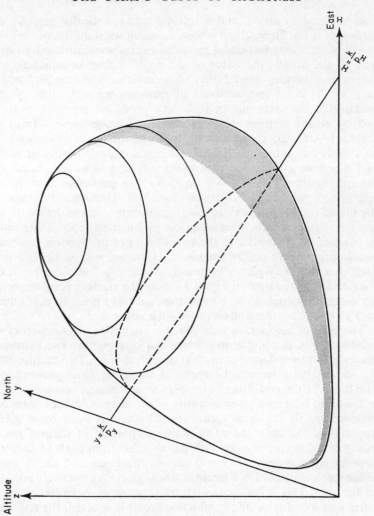

The production hill seen in perspective.

Quantities of factor x are measured on the west–east axis, and of factor y on the north–south axis. Output is measured on the altitude axis z. The budget line, running from $y = k/p_y$ on the y-axis to $x = k/p_x$ on the x-axis, shows all pairs of quantities (x,y) which can be hired with a constant weekly expenditure k when their prices are constant at p_x and p_y.

The profile of a vertical section, outlined in dashes, through the hill along the budget line, shows by its point of tangency with an equal-output curve or contour line the pair of quantities (x,y) which gives the greatest output for expenditure k.

FIG. 3.3.

53

lines referred to above, and a section made vertically downwards through the hill along a line whose meaning we shall discuss below.

Although it may be helpful to visualize the production-hill in this way 'in the round', the virtue of the contour lines or equal-output curves is that they render this unnecessary. Selecting any point (x,y) in the north-east quadrant at random, we seek other points which give the same output (quantity produced per time-unit) z, and by means of these we trace an *equal-output curve* z $(x,y) =$ constant. Alternatively we can go to work the other way round. If we specify z as some particular number, say z_1, any particular value of x which we may choose at random will have to be associated, on the equal-output curve $z_1 = z$ (x,y) for this particular z, with the appropriate value of y to satisfy this equation. Thus once the shape of the hill of production is given, any equal-output curve drawn on its surface implies a rule of association (a function) connecting with each other the quantities of the two factors of production. Such an equal-output curve can be imagined as drawn, not on the hill-side itself, but in the xy-plane. Moreover, since any and every point of the north-east quadrant of Fig. 3.3 can be the starting point for tracing an equal output curve, we must regard *every* point in that quadrant as lying on some one or other such curve.

The type of association between the quantities of two factors of production on an equal-output curve can vary between two extremes according to their degree of mutual substitutability. Two factors may for technological reasons be required in rigidly fixed proportions, like those of the constituent elements in a chemical compound. Or at the other extreme a given quantity of one may in all circumstances produce exactly the same technological effect as some other given quantity of the other, as when some proportion of natural gas is burnt in a domestic cooker with gas distilled from coal. In the first case the equal-output curve will consist effectively of a single point at the meeting place of two straight-line segments respectively parallel to the axes. This is because, with *fixed technical coefficients*, once a particular quantity of one productive factor is selected, the required quantity of the other is also fixed, and no matter how great the quantity employed of that other factor, it will make no difference to the output. In the second case, the equal-output curve will be a straight line sloping down from left to right, indicating that some given reduction in the quantity employed of one factor can everywhere be precisely compensated by one and the same increment of the quantity employed of the other. The literature of economics has usually assumed these two extreme cases to be untypical. The usual case is supposed to lie between them. It is supposed that the effectiveness of one factor as a substitute for the other will decline as the proportion of the former increases. In farming, for example, the same quantity of crop may be obtained from a smaller acreage more intensively cultivated, but each superimposed reduction by one acre will require a larger increase in man-hours of work on the remaining acres to compensate it, than its predecessors did. The equal-output curve will in such cases slope down from left to right with numerically decreasing steepness, bending more and more towards the horizontal and thus being convex towards the origin, as in Fig. 3.4. It will thus

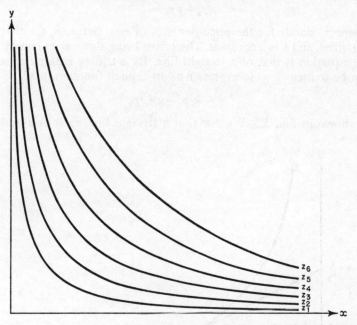

Equal-output curves are labelled z_1, z_2, . . ., they are specimens from an infinite family of such curves, densely covering the whole north-east quadrant for all relevant or practicable numerical values of x and y.

FIG. 3.4

be possible for a straight line to have one, but only one, point of tangency with such an equal-output curve. Fig. 3.3 can, of course, show only a few specimen curves out of the infinitely many which we must imagine to cover the north-east quadrant in such a way that every point in that quadrant (or at least its relevant region) lies on one such curve. As we follow a straight line from the origin into the north-eastern quadrant, we shall reach points which successively represent larger quantities of both factors of production and which will accordingly be associated with larger and larger outputs. The further from the origin an equal-output curve lies, along such a line through the origin, the greater the output it represents.

A budget line consists of all those points (x, y) each of which, considered as a pair of quantities of two factors of production, has some one and the same given money cost. If the market price per unit of each factor is given, a budget line will be a straight line sloping downwards from left to right. For our definition of it can be written algebraically

$$xp_x + yp_y = k$$

where p_x stands for the price per unit of one factor, p_y for that of the other, and k is a constant. The prices being themselves constants, the equation is that of a straight line. By a trifling manipulation it can be written so as to express y as an explicit function of x:

$$y = k/p_y - xp_x/p_y$$

as shown in Fig. 3.5. We saw that a straight line, such as a budget

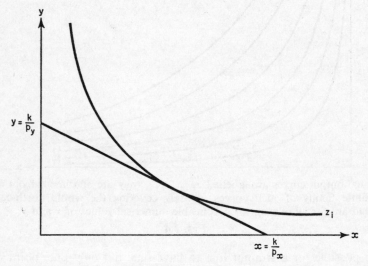

The budget line is a segment of the straight line $xp_x + yp_y = k$. It is the segment cut off by the two axes at the intercepts, namely the point $y = k/p_y$ on y-axis and $x = k/p_x$ on the x-axis. z_i is that one of the equal-output curves which is tangent to the budget line.

FIG. 3.5

line, can have one but only one point of tangency with an equal-output curve. This fact enables us to answer the question: When some one equal-output curve is selected, what will be the cheapest combination of quantities of the two factors, capable of producing that output?

By assigning a different total expenditure, say m, for the two factors of production taken together, we get a differently positioned, but parallel, budget line. At each greater value of k, m, etc., the corresponding budget line will lie above and to the right of the others, and we can thus find one which has a point of tangency with our chosen equal-output curve. This point of tangency will show the cheapest combination of quantities of the two factors which is able to produce the output in question. For a budget line below and to the left of the tangent line has no point in common with the chosen equal-output curve, while a budget line above and to the right of the tangent line represents combinations of quantities costing, as a pair, more than those on the tangent line.

The same proposition can be established algebraically. Let us suppose ourselves to follow a path across that 'output-hill' whose shape is shown by the contour lines or equal-output curves, along a course traced by the tangent budget line. We shall thus at first ascend and later descend the shoulder of the hill. Our altitude at any point (x, y) will be given by the expression for the production function whose shape the hill represents:

$$z = z(x, y) \tag{3.1}$$

So long as we confine ourselves to the budget line, x and y are not free to vary independently of each other, but stand, as we have seen, in a relation which we can write

$$y = y(x) \tag{3.2}$$

Combining equations (3.1) and (3.2) we have an expression for the profile of the hill which would be revealed if we sliced it vertically downwards along the course of the budget line:

$$z = z\{x, y(x)\}$$

which tells us that z depends directly on x, and also on y which itself depends on x. We can now differentiate with respect to x:

$$\frac{dz}{dx} = \frac{\partial z}{\partial x} + \frac{\partial z}{\partial y} \frac{dy}{dx}$$

The highest point of the path over the hill will be that where the derivative is zero:

$$\frac{\partial z}{\partial x} + \frac{\partial z}{\partial y} \frac{dy}{dx} = 0$$

or

$$\frac{dy}{dx} = -\frac{\partial z}{\partial x} \bigg/ \frac{\partial z}{\partial y} \qquad (3.3)$$

When we look back at our expression for a contour line, we find that this same relation, which holds at only one point of the budget line profile of the hill, holds everywhere along the contour line or equal-output curve. We have seen that every point of the north-east quadrant lies on some equal-output curve, and therefore the highest point of the profile, given by our equation (3.3) does so too. But when we consider the equal-output curve as a function relating x and y, and the budget line as another such function, we now see that at the top of the budget line profile of the hill, they have the same derivative of y with respect to x, namely

$$\frac{dy}{dx} = -\frac{\partial z}{\partial x} \bigg/ \frac{\partial z}{\partial y}$$

Thus at the one point which the budget line and the contour line have in common, namely at the highest point on the hill which can be attained without leaving the budget-line path, these two curves are parallel, and therefore tangent.

This rather barren-looking formal fact has an important economic interpretation. The intercept of the budget line on the y-axis (the distance of their meeting point from the origin) represents the quantity of factor y which could be employed if the whole expenditure which the budget line allows for both factors together, k, was spent on y alone. Similarly the intercept on the x-axis shows how much x could be employed if all of k were spent on x. Thus the ratio of the two intercepts is the price-ratio of the two factors. If the y-intercept is twice the x-intercept, this means that the price of a unit of x is twice that of a unit of y (since only half as many units of x, as of y, can be bought with a given sum of money). Thus we have the result that a given output can be most cheaply produced by such a pair of factor-quantities that a little extra of one can make good a small loss of the other without altering output or total cost.

The terminology of *marginal quantities* and *marginal curves*, though it expresses no more than the simplest notions of the differential calculus, will be essential to us in what follows, because of its established use in economics and its word-saving compactness. A marginal quantity is simply a difference between two values of a variable. It is of no interest by itself, but only when compared with that difference, with which some function associates it, of another variable. In forming a difference-quotient or derivative, we divide a difference of the dependent variable by a difference of the independent variable. Since economists often set the latter difference equal to one unit, division by which leaves the dividend (the numerator) unchanged, the habit has arisen of referring to marginal product, marginal cost, and so on, without specifying in each case what other (independent) variable is involved. Our proposition above can be rephrased. Production of a given output will be cheapest when such factor-quantities are employed that marginal quantities, which can exactly compensate each other in production, have the same cost. We realize that a budget line could be called a *constant-cost curve*.

A change in the ratio of the prices of the factors will evidently change the factor-quantities which are cheapest for a given output. A new budget line, with a new slope representing the new price-ratio of the factors, will be tangent to the chosen equal-output curve at a different point from the former tangency. Our argument in this section may seem too much simplified and remote from reality to throw light on real questions. Yet it proves one important truth. The question how a given output can be most cheaply produced cannot be answered from 'engineering' knowledge alone. Knowledge of the prices and supply conditions of factors is on the same footing of importance.

5. SCALE

If it were the case that the output of some product depended solely on the quantities employed of two means of production and on no other circumstances; and if each of these factor-quantities could be changed by as small a difference as we liked; then there is no evident reason why the function associating pairs (x,y) of these factor-quantities with the output z should not be such as to give *constant returns to scale*, so that if the quantity employed of every factor were changed in some given ratio, the output would thereby be changed in the same ratio. A production function having this character is called by the mathematicians linear and homogeneous, but we can visualize it as a surface such that a straight-edge pivoted at the origin could be made to lie in contact with the surface from the origin to any point on the surface in the 'north-east' region where both factor-quantities are positive. Constant returns to scale are not, of course, limited to the case of only two factors, and though we cannot have a visual image of a function involving more than three variables in all, the production function can be linear and homogeneous with any number of factors. When *every* circumstance which can affect production has been included in the list of factors of production, and is found to be measurable in some readily apprehended unit and also perfectly divisible, a very important consequence follows concerning the sharing out of the income earned by the production and sale of the product. But we have to ask whether this complete measurability and divisibility of the circumstances of production is realistic.

We defined the firm's purpose as that of making as large as possible the excess of the value of its outputs over that of its inputs. We are for the present confining ourselves to the short-period aspect of that purpose, and to the case where the firm makes only one kind of product (that is, in the terminology of activity analysis, one output) though it uses several distinct means of production or inputs. The short-period problem is that in which the firm already possesses some block of apparatus, or has already engaged some cadre of highly qualified persons, whose size, in the sense of the weekly or daily quantity and the quality of the services this apparatus or cadre can render, is fixed for the time being. Now this fixity of the employed quantity of a means of production does not, of course, conform to the conditions in which we said that the production function would represent *constant returns to scale*. The 'fixed factor' cannot change in the same proportion as the other factors; it cannot change at all. There are then two possibilities. The fixed factor may leave the other factors quite unaffected in their productive performance, beyond making that performance possible by its presence, as a mixing bowl does not affect the way in which the ingredients of a cake contribute to its making, beyond allowing them to be mixed together. Or a change in the proportion of the variable factors to the fixed factor may influence the effectiveness of all these factors taken together, just as a change in the proportion of the variable factors amongst themselves would do. In the 'mixing bowl' case the variable factors considered by themselves may conform to a linear homogeneous production function, so that when they are all increased in one and the same proportion, the output is increased in that same proportion. In the other case, it is likely that superimposed equal increments of the variable group will raise the output at first by increasing and then by decreasing steps, until at some point the variable group becomes absolutely excessive for the fixed factor and begins even to cause a decrease of output. Artisans in a workshop, when their numbers are too few to permit full specialization, will become more efficient as their numbers increase. But eventually the growing numbers will overcrowd and impede one another. Figure 3.6 shows this effect by means of a Knightian curve, so called after the famous American economist Frank H. Knight. Let a surface $z = z(x,y)$ show the output resulting from the combination of quantities x and y with each other and with some fixed quantity of a third factor. This third factor need not appear in our geometry at all, except by its effect on the performance of the other factors. We

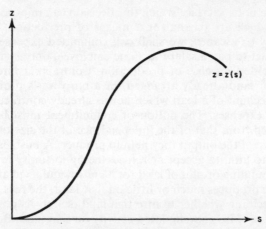

A Knightian curve associating sizes z of output with quantities s of two factors combined in fixed proportions.

FIG. 3.6

now cut downwards through the output-hill at right angles to the xy-plane along a straight line through the origin, points on which line will evidently represent combinations of x and y in some constant proportion to each other. The profile of this section, the curve in which the vertical section-plane meets the surface of the hill, is a Knightian curve. It shows the effect on output of scale-increases of the variable factors. As we move towards the right from the origin, the curve $z = z(s)$, where s stands for numbers of units of a factor composed of x and y in fixed proportions, slopes up at first with increasing and then with decreasing steepness until it reaches the top of the profile and begins to descend. It shows at first increasing returns to scale and then decreasing returns to scale, where 'scale' refers to the variable factors only.

6. COSTS

The production-function describes production possibilities in terms of physical quantities of factors and products. But the firm's concern is with market values. From production possibilities we must therefore proceed to costs (priced inputs) and revenues (priced outputs). The costs of executing some plan are the payments which cannot be avoided if the plan is to be executed, but which will be avoided if the plan is abandoned. Payments which you are already committed to make, and must make regardless of what you now decide to do, are of course a part of the circumstances and background of that decision, but they are not a sacrifice which this decision can impose upon you. Expenses which are paying for a means of production, but which cannot now be escaped, we shall call committed expenses. A long-term contract to pay a salary to some employee, once signed, would be a committed expense of production. Contractual hire of plant, buildings or land already arranged, or a borrower's promised payments on account of a loan which he has already contracted for, are committed expenses. The notion of commitment must be carefully distinguished from that of the independence of the size of payments from the size of the output they help to produce. A businessman may have open to him, to accept or refuse, the opportunity to hire some particular building or plot of land for a known and fixed annual rent. Whether he produces much or little on that land, the rent will be the same. In deciding whether to hire that land or not, its rent comes in now as a cost of his contemplated activity on that land. But once the contract is signed, it ceases to be a cost of that activity. However, even before the contract is signed, the rent of the land is different from the payments he will have to make for materials to form the substance of his product, or which are to provide power for his machines. For the weekly or annual size of these latter expenses will depend on the size of his output.

We come back, then, to the distinction between the short and the long period. When a businessman looks beyond his immediate future, to a time when his existing plant will need replacing and his existing contracts will have run out, he is looking to a state of freedom, when everything he now decides to do implies some sacrifice of what might have been done instead. All the payments, in that long-period perspective, are costs. The short period, by contrast, is that in which some of the physical frame of his productive activity cannot be changed, and also that in which some of his payments are the subject of contracts that have still some time to run, and thus have ceased to be costs. Long-period production decisions are really investment decisions, decisions as to what products to make and what markets to enter, what durable plant to set up; in short, what kind of new business to establish or into what new channels to steer the activity of an existing one. Investment decisions are the subject matter of the chapters which follow this one. Here we shall still confine ourselves to the short period.

In the short period the firm is not choosing a production function, but choosing whereabouts to place itself on a function whose shape has been set by the firm's past decisions concerning what equipment to buy and what specialized staff to engage. Let us suppose that the expense for this equipment and the salaries of this staff have already been contracted for and now lie outside the firm's field of choice.

The production function will now express the relation between those factors of production which the firm has still to hire or buy, and the size of the output these will be able, with the aid of the 'fixed' equipment and specialized staff, to produce. We have shown in basic principle how, given such a function, the firm can select, for any chosen output of any specified product, the set of quantities of means of production which will produce this output most cheaply. Let us remind ourselves that such a function is an expression of technological knowledge, and that the budget line is an expression of market knowledge. To assume that the firm can guide its actions by this apparatus is to assume that, in effect, all this knowledge is available to it. Our chief task in later chapters will be to examine the consequences of dispensing with such assumptions, or to consider in what precise sense they can be treated as fulfilled. Having assumed that the firm possesses this knowledge, we are compelled to suppose that it makes use of it, for the economist's essential subject matter is the interaction of need, circumstance and reason. He makes no claim to understand conduct emancipated from reason. We assume, then, that for any output, the firm will choose the cheapest combination of factors open to it. Measuring output on the east–west axis of Fig. 3.7, we measure northwards for each output the total cost of the freely choosable factors needed for it, obtained by multiplying the number of units employed of each factor by its price per unit, and adding together the resulting factor-bills. If the variable factors are perfectly divisible, and if their effectiveness over some range of outputs is independent of the relation of their quantity to the size of the 'fixed' apparatus (that is, if the latter has only the mixing-bowl duty) the total cost-curve will be a sloping straight line extending to that output where the 'mixing bowl' is full, whence it will rise vertically, indicating that no extra output can be obtained at any cost. If the efficiency of the variable factors is affected by their relation to the fixed apparatus, the total cost-curve will not be straight over any range of output, but may, for example, be concave downwards over small outputs and concave upwards over larger ones, as in Fig. 3.7.

The relation of cost to output can be expressed by each of two other curves, each having its own useful application. If we plot against output the *derivative* of total costs with respect to output, we have the *marginal cost curve*. Each ordinate, or 'northwards' distance of this curve from the east–west axis, shows, for the output concerned, the *extra* cost that one extra unit of output would involve. The marginal and total cost-curves are, of course, rigidly related to each other. Where the total cost-curve is concave towards the east–west axis, that is, where its slope decreases as output increases, the

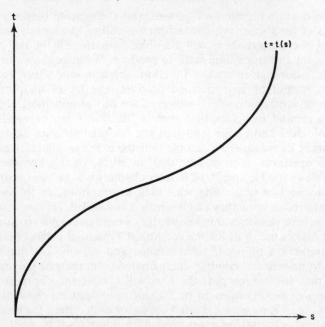

Ordinates of the curve $t = t(s)$ show for each output s the total cost t of the variable factors of production.

FIG. 3.7

marginal cost-curve slopes downward (southwards). Where the total curve has a constant slope, the marginal curve has a constant northwards distance. Where the total cost-curve is concave northwards, the marginal curve slopes up. Thirdly we come to the *average cost curve*, each of whose ordinates is obtained by dividing the total cost of any output by that output. Let t stand for the total cost of output s. Then average cost u is $u = t(s)/s$ and if average cost has a minimum this will be where $du/ds = 0$. We have

$$\frac{du}{ds} = \frac{1}{s^2}\left(s\frac{dt}{ds} - t\right) = \frac{1}{s}\left(\frac{dt}{ds} - \frac{t}{s}\right)$$

and this will be equal to zero where $dt/ds = t/s$, that is, where marginal cost equals average cost. Over that range of output where $dt/ds < t/s$ (where marginal cost is less than average cost), the derivative of average cost with respect to output is negative; that is to say, the average cost-curve will be sloping downwards from west to east.

64

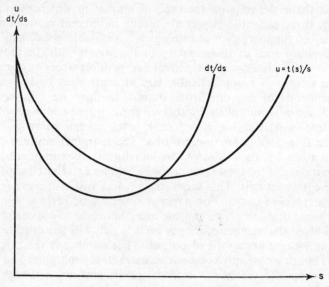

$u = t(s)/s$ is average or unit cost;
dt/ds is marginal cost.

FIG. 3.8

Where $dt/ds > t/s$, average cost will be increasing with output. Thus the marginal and average cost-curves will be related as in Fig. 3.8, with the marginal curve cutting the average curve from below at the latter's minimum.

7. REVENUE

Revenue is the number of money-units received by the firm in a week or a year from the sale of its product. This number is equal to the number of units of product sold per time-unit multiplied by the price per unit. It is a flow, like the output for which it is given in exchange. The price per unit must in general be looked on as a function of the output, and so, of course, must the firm's revenue. The function connecting revenue with output can be represented by the same three types of curve as the function connecting costs with output, and by drawing these two sets of curves on one diagram we can show how the firm should determine its output. Its aim in the framework of its short-period circumstances is to make as large as it can, by suitable choice of the size of its output, the excess of total revenue over total cost. To show the firm's test of success in this endeavour, we must first consider the shape of the revenue-curves.

This shape depends on the type of market in which the firm is selling. If the potential buyers are totally indifferent between a vast number of suppliers of a technologically definable good, and these suppliers are each of them small in comparison with the group of suppliers as a whole, we have perfect competition where any firm can sell an output of any practicable size at a price set by the market independently of any one firm's output. In this case total revenue will be output multiplied by this uniform price, and with output measured on the east–west axis, the total revenue-curve will be a straight line sloping north-eastwards. The marginal revenue-curve, representing by its *ordinates* (its northward measurements) this *constant slope* of the total revenue-curve, will be a straight line parallel to the east–west axis. This same straight line will also serve for the average revenue-curve. For average revenue, or *revenue per unit*, is the same thing as price, and the marginal revenue-curve shows at each output the number of money units which will be added to total revenue by one extra unit of output. That number is the price per unit. Thus in a perfectly competitive market, the marginal and average revenue-curves are one and the same, and are a straight line parallel to the east–west or output axis.

When buyers, for any reason, have a preference for particular firms, some for one firm and some for another, the price which a firm receives per unit of product will depend on the number of units of product it puts on the market per week or year. If it raises its price, it will not lose all its buyers to other firms selling an identical product, for by assumption there are no such firms. Each firm is in a sense the *sole* seller of its own product, since that product has attached to it, in the eyes of at least some buyers, a special quality which is peculiar to the firm in question. For the same reason it cannot engross the entire market by lowering its price below that of other firms, for some of their customers will remain loyal to them. In this case of *imperfect* or *monopolistic* competition, the firm's average revenue-curve will slope south-eastwards, not necessarily in a straight line, but everywhere associating a fall in price with an increase in quantity sold. The average revenue-curve means many things, and for each such aspect of it we have a special name. We can call it the price-curve or the demand-curve facing the firm. For it expresses not only the price per unit which the firm can charge when it wishes to sell a given output, but also the inverse of this, namely the demand which will be elicited by a given price. When the firm moves to a different point on its average revenue-curve by, for example, lowering its price, it will be selling not only the extra units now demanded, but its entire output, at a lower price than was charged before. Thus this move will have two effects. It will increase the quantity sold per unit of time, and reduce the price. What will be the effect on total revenue? This depends on, or reflects, an important characteristic of the demand-curve facing the firm, called *price elasticity of demand*.

Let us write p for the number of money units received for each unit of product (the price) and x for the number of units of product demanded per unit of time (the demand). Then revenue r, will be

$$r = px$$

Will px be bigger or smaller when p is reduced by a small amount $-\Delta p$? This depends on whether the corresponding increase in x, Δx, bears a larger or smaller relation to x than Δp does to p. If x increases in a larger proportion than p decreases, px will get bigger. We define the price elasticity of demand as the ratio of these two proportions, that is

$$\eta = \frac{\Delta x}{x} \bigg/ \frac{\Delta p}{p}$$

This is evidently the same as $(\Delta x/\Delta p)(p/x)$, which we can write in the limit (that is, letting Δp tend to zero) $dx/dp)(p/x)$.

Marginal revenue in principle is the difference between two terms of opposite algebraic sign. One of these terms represents the gain of revenue due to an increase in quantity sold, the other is the loss of revenue due to the selling of the whole output at a lower price than formerly. In fact we have according to the rule for differentiating the product of two functions of the same independent variable

$$\frac{dr}{dx} = \frac{d}{dx}(px)$$

$$= \frac{dp}{dx}x + \frac{dx}{dx}p$$

$$= \frac{dp}{dx}x + p \tag{3.4}$$

The price elasticity of demand, we saw, is $(dx/dp)(p/x)$, and the reciprocal of this (the result of using it as denominator of a fraction whose numerator is *one*) is

$$\frac{1}{\eta} = \frac{dp}{dx}\frac{x}{p}.$$

If we multiply this reciprocal by p (by crossing p out from the denominator) we have the first term in our expression for marginal revenue, and that expression can accordingly be written

$$\frac{dr}{dx} = \frac{1}{\eta}p + p$$

$$= p\left(1 + \frac{1}{\eta}\right) \qquad (3.5)$$

So long as the average revenue-curve associates an increase or positive change dx in quantity sold with a decrease or negative change dp in price, the ratio of these two, dx/dp, will be negative, and so therefore will the elasticity $(dx/dp)(p/x)$ and its reciprocal. Thus the term $1 + 1/\eta$ will be less than unity, and equation (3.5) above tells us that price will be everywhere greater than marginal revenue except at zero output, $x = 0$.

There is no reason at all to suppose that the demand-curve facing a firm, if its shape could be discovered, would be a straight line. But in fact any special shape we may give it, for the purpose of an illustrative diagram, will be quite arbitrary. A straight line will therefore serve, and this simplifies the plotting of the corresponding marginal revenue-curve, which will then itself be a straight line sloping to a point on the east–west or output axis which is just half way between the origin and the intercept of the average revenue-curve on that axis. This is illustrated in Fig. 3.9.

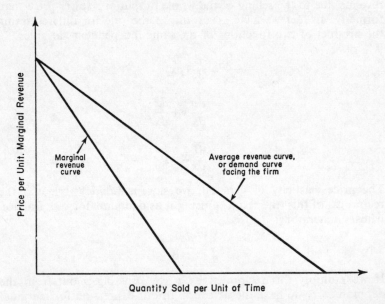

Marginal revenue curve

Average revenue curve, or demand curve facing the firm

Quantity Sold per Unit of Time

Price per Unit. Marginal Revenue

Fig. 3.9

8. THE TEST OF GREATEST NET REVENUE

Before we show how the apparatus of cost- and revenue-curves fixes the output which will make the excess of total revenue over total cost as large as possible in the firm's short-period circumstances, let us insist again on the formal character of this apparatus and its nature of a means of expressing facts if those facts can be discovered, rather than a prime source of readily available knowledge. The conception of a market where tastes, incomes, rival products and, above all, expectations concerning these things, remain unchanged while the firm varies the price of its product experimentally over a wide range in order to map out a demand-curve conforming to the ideal definition, can scarcely exist even in logic, let alone reality. However, the firm's practical concern at any moment is with only a small range of its conceptual demand-curve, in the close neighbourhood of the price it is actually charging. What it particularly needs to know is how the actual elasticity of demand at that price compares with an elasticity of unity. If the elasticity is numerically small, it may pay the firm to raise its price by steps until the elasticity has considerably increased. The relation of costs to output will be easier to ascertain than that of demand. Our purpose now is to show what formal use the firm should make of the information or conjectures it can reach concerning the two sets of conditions.

The firm's net revenue, v, is the difference between its revenue $p(s)s$, of an output s sold at a price $p(s)$ per unit (this price itself, as our notation indicates, being a function of the output), and the total cost $t = t(s)$ of this output. We remember that s, t and v are all of them flows, numbers of physical or money units per unit of time. Thus we have

$$v = p(s)s - t(s)$$

Differentiating this with respect to s we have

$$\frac{dv}{ds} = \frac{dp}{ds}s + p - \frac{dt}{ds}$$

which reads 'marginal net revenue equals marginal revenue, namely $s\,dp/ds + p$, minus marginal cost, dt/ds. To determine the (algebraic, not monetary) value of s which makes v a maximum, we put dv/ds equal to zero, so that

$$\frac{dp}{ds}s + p - \frac{dt}{ds} = 0$$

or

$$\frac{dp}{ds}s + p = \frac{dt}{ds}$$

'marginal revenue equals marginal cost'. This is the condition first stated in a slightly different form by Augustin Cournot in 1838, for the firm to attain its maximum net revenue.

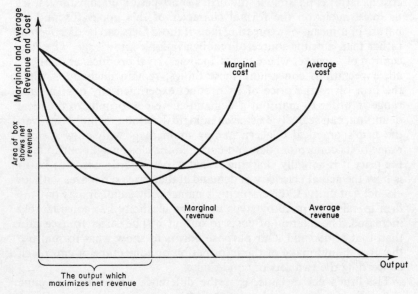

FIG. 3.10

Figure 3.10 shows the marginal and average revenue-curves and the marginal and average cost-curves of some firm. On this diagram, let us imagine a straight line which remains parallel to the north–south axis, but is capable of being bodily shifted eastwards or westwards. Let it at first coincide with the north–south axis, and then move eastwards by steps each representing one unit of output. When this line has taken up a position a few units to the east of the origin, we move northwards along this line. Taking notice at first of the marginal curves only, we come first to the marginal cost-curve and then to the marginal revenue-curve. Each unit of output which the eastward shifting of the line has so far superimposed one on another has therefore added more to total revenue than it has to total cost. For the marginal curves show, respectively, the number of money units added to total revenue or total cost by one extra unit of output superimposed on some attained size of output. As the northward-pointing line shifts eastward step by step, it will eventually come to that size of output where the two marginal curves intersect each other. Eastward of that point, the marginal revenue-curve lies nearer the output-axis than the marginal cost-curve does. Thus, eastward of that point, each eastward step adds more to total cost than it adds to total revenue. For greatest *net* revenue, the line should have stopped its eastward movement at the point of intersection, *where marginal cost and marginal revenue are equal.*

Let us look now at the 'average' curves. Our shiftable northward-pointing line, stationed where it runs through the intersection-point of marginal revenue and marginal cost, brings us first, as we move northward along it, to the average cost-curve and then to the average revenue-curve. The northwards distance between these curves represents the difference between the price and the cost of a unit of product. When we multiply the number of money units of net revenue per unit of product by the number of weekly (yearly, etc.) units of product, we get the firm's weekly or yearly net revenue. That net revenue is thus represented on our diagram by the *area* of the rectangle whose adjacent sides are respectively the northward distance between the two 'average' curves and the eastward distance of the shiftable vertical line from the origin, since this latter distance represents the output. The net revenue, at its greatest possible, attained by choosing that output which equalizes marginal revenue and marginal cost, is represented also by the area enclosed between the northward axis and the two marginal curves as far as their intersection.

What considerations suggest or justify our giving Fig. 3.10 the type of pattern that it shows? In particular, why have we made marginal revenues exceed marginal costs over some range of outputs from zero to a point of intersection, beyond which marginal costs exceed marginal revenues? Why does the average cost-curve, as we move eastwards from a zero output, at first decline towards lower average cost and then begin to rise? Is net revenue bound to be greater than zero? Taking the last of these questions first, let us consider a situation (Fig. 3.11) where the average cost-curve has a point of tangency with the average revenue-curve. The net revenue rectangle of Fig. 3.10 will here have shrunk to a single line and vanished. The firm's net revenue will be zero, but this will still be the largest net revenue it can attain. For at any other output than the one corresponding to the point of tangency, average cost will be greater than average revenue. In still another situation, the firm, studying its circumstances before deciding upon its output, might find that every output led to a *negative* net revenue. The rectangle of net revenue would reappear but, no matter what output was chosen, its northward-pointing side would represent an excess of average cost over average revenue. In such circumstances, the firm would no doubt decide to produce nothing. Thus in giving the

71

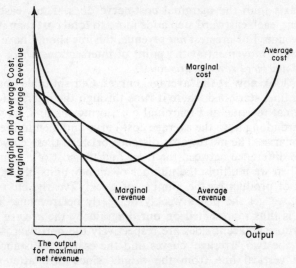

FIG. 3.11

marginal curves the relation we have shown in Figs. 3.10 and 3.11 we are merely taking that case where the firm will have some incentive to produce a greater than zero output.

We have answered the first and third of our questions. The second has been answered already in our discussions of the meaning of the short period and the effect of non-variable factors of production. The shape we have given the average cost-curve corresponds to the supposition that when relatively very small quantities of variable factors are combined with a large block of equipment or of natural resources, their efficiency is low, perhaps because of the restricted scope for specialization or 'division of labour'. As the quantities of the variable factors are increased, their efficiency at first increases, but eventually it must decline again as the unchanging frame of apparatus or of land within which they work begins to cramp them and to offer only tasks of less and less usefulness for extra workers to perform, or less and less adequate sustenance for livestock, and so on.

Let us now revert to the question of the applicability of these logical principles. The principles themselves, though concerned with relations between quantities, are in a sense merely classificatory. They show why the average cost-curve may often be U-shaped, but they tell us little about its precise form. When the role of the fixed factor is that of a mere mixing bowl, the efficiency of a given combination of quantities of the variable factors could be constant over a range of output from zero up to some absolute stop, representing, as it were, the point where the bowl will not hold any more ingredients. Or it may be that, though the curve is in principle roughly U-shaped, the segment of it which slopes south-eastward is the practically important part, so that the cost of variable factors per unit of output declines over a large range and then climbs abruptly. A curve of this general shape would justify the frequent public references which are made to the need for keeping industrial plants working 'near to capacity' in order that costs may be low.

9. OVERHEADS

Let us remind ourselves of two categories which are in essence quite separate ideas, but which are linked by the practice and institutions of the business world. *Committed expenses* are those outlays of money to which the firm is already committed before it begins to consider how large an output to produce. *Fixed factors of production* are those blocks of equipment or of natural resources, employed or contemplated for purchase by the firm, whose size cannot be varied within the short period which is our present concern. The link between these two categories is the fact that committed expenses have usually been undertaken in order to secure the possession or use of blocks of equipment or of land.

We saw that, in any particular situation, those expenses which the firm can no longer legally avoid are not costs of whatever it may decide, in this situation, to do, though the necessity of making these payments may, of course, restrict its field of choice by reducing its resources. We have been studying the *short period* in the sense of a situation where the firm possesses some fixed factors of production and is already committed to paying for them, and has now only to decide what quantities of variable factors to hire for the purpose of exploiting these fixed factors. Now let us suppose, instead, that the firm has still to provide itself with equipment or with land, and that this factor can only be obtained in large blocks widely different in size, but that this factor and the perfectly variable factors can all be the subject of contracts covering one and the same length of time ahead. In these days of plant-hire companies, our suppositions can be illustrated by the case of drag-lines available in many different, but widely spaced, sizes, which can be hired for a month at a time. The firm's production problem now involves it in choosing what size of the block-factor to acquire, having regard to the largest net revenue which can be obtained from each size of block by the right choice of output for that particular size of block. Net revenue, however, must under these new suppositions be reckoned by *in-*

cluding amongst costs the expense of the block factor, for we are supposing this expense to be still subject to choice. How is this expense to be included in the analysis?

The choice of any one size of block will superimpose, on whatever amount is paid for variable factors, an amount which will be one and the same, unchanging, no matter what output is produced with the help of that particular size of block. Such an expense, whose amount is independent of the amount produced with its aid, is called an *overhead* cost. Let us remind ourselves of our assumption that all factors, including the block-factor, are hired or bought so as to provide for production during one and the same period ahead. We can still, therefore, regard the expenses for all of them as so-and-so much per unit of time. And since we are studying the firm's calculations while it is still free to sign or not sign contracts for these outlays, all of them are costs. If the overhead cost is a fixed amount K and the output produced with its aid a variable s, the share of overhead ascribable to each unit of output will be $c = K/s$. The curve representing c as a function of s will be a rectangular hyperbola as illustrated in Fig. 3.12 and c will be the unit overhead cost or average fixed cost of the product. What will be the marginal cost of the block of equipment of fixed size and fixed expense? It will be zero. The

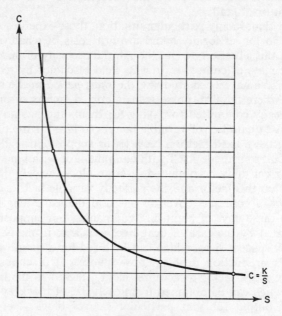

FIG. 3.12

derivative of any quantity, with respect to a variable of which that quantity is *independent*, is zero. Thus there is no marginal overhead cost-curve, or if we insist on having one, it will have to coincide with the axis of output so as to be zero for all outputs. All we need do, therefore, to include overhead cost in our general diagram is to draw in the curve $c = K/s$, the average overhead cost-curve, and add the ordinates or northward distances of this curve from the output axis to those of the average variable cost-curve to get an average combined cost-curve. Everything included in this latter will be a genuine cost, because we are supposing the firm to have still the freedom of choice between making this outlay and not making it.

Now for *each* size of the block-factor, the firm will have a distinct marginal cost-curve for variable factors needed to exploit this block of equipment. This is so because any given set of quantities of the variable factors will produce a different output when they are combined with a different block of equipment. Each such relevant marginal cost-curve will have a point of intersection with the marginal revenue-curve. At this best output for the corresponding size of the block-factor, the firm can (on our present supposition that it possesses all relevant knowledge) subtract the average combined cost from the average revenue of that output, and multiply the resulting average *net* revenue by the output to find the net revenue obtainable with that size of equipment. From amongst the net revenue sizes corresponding to various sizes of block it can choose the largest.

The frame of suppositions whose consequences we have been analysing in this section hitherto is a most uninteresting one. We have in fact deliberately assumed away all those circumstances which present difficulty and introduce any useful extension of the firm's production problem. In particular, we have carefully excluded the essence of the firm's *long-period* problem, that of *investment*, and even in the short-period setting, we have avoided the question of firms (which in practice include all real firms) that produce a variety of distinct products. For when the same mixing bowl can be used for a variety of cakes, we cannot say, on any logical ground, how much of the expense of the mixing bowl should be borne by any one kind of cake. The problem of what equipment it will best pay the firm to buy can be solved, in principle, only by considering every rival set of outputs which it would be possible for each conceivable type and size of equipment to produce. Moreover, a piece of equipment (a plant, machine or building) promises service for many times as long as the usual contract period for hiring labour, which may be a month or a week. Thus the firm must try to form some conception of the possible net revenue from such a piece of equipment far into future years, and in deciding whether or not to buy that equipment, it must remember that its suppositions about their net revenues are, in essence, figments and not facts. They are not *fictions* in the sense of mental creations unrelated to contemporary evidence concerning the perceived world. But they are intellectual constructs only founded on, and not guaranteed by, such evidence. They are highly, and irredeemably, uncertain.

Business success today springs largely from successful innovation. The very concept of *novelty* implies essential and deep-rooted uncertainty, for the novel is the hitherto unknown, even the unimagined. If there can be new knowledge, there must have been either wrong knowledge or a gap in knowledge. In either case an awareness of the possibility that accepted knowledge is wrong or is insufficient is precisely what we mean by uncertainty. The need for a means of expressing uncertainty and giving it recognition and an explicit and insistent role in business policy-formation and policy-revision will be the concern of Chapters 5 and 6. First, however, in Chapter 4, we shall state formally the problem of investment. In this foregoing chapter we have carefully avoided that problem, confining ourselves to the short period in which the relevant investment has either already been done or else is placed, unrealistically, within the same short-period frame as the purchase of 'variable' factors.

The formulation of the long-period problem as that of investment turns the notion of overhead costs upside down. Investment in some item or system of equipment is only worth while in so far as there seems to be a possibility that the sale of the output produced with its aid will leave enough trading revenue over, after paying for the co-operating or 'variable' factors, to pay back the sum which will have to be invested in that equipment after allowing for the deferment of those trading revenues. The analysis of all this is the object of our next three chapters.

CHAPTER 4

Investment

1. DURABILITY

Durable facilities of production face the businessman with peculiar difficulties of decision. The value to him of such a tool is in origin the value it can add to his output. But since it is durable, its promised services stretch over many future years. In those years of unknown conditions and events, what will its service be worth? In principle the businessman who has a fortune at command ought to pass in review all imaginable products and all imaginable systems of facilities for producing each such product, and choose what he has some ground for supposing to be the most profitable. This is a manifold impossibility. It is impossible because the task of imagination would be endless, and take endless time, and would thus be fruitless. It is impossible because the question what is most profitable can only be answered if the businessman knows what others are themselves imagining and proposing, and what they will conceive of in future, and those things are at least unknown to him, and some of them unknowable to anyone. In practice his task is simpler. He has some preference or experience of his own, and perhaps some existing facilities, for making a particular product. His field of choice may thus be naturally circumscribed at the outset. But within that delimited field, and even within the further circumscribed list of already existing designs of tools fit for his productive purpose, his task of valuation of each design and scale of plant or equipment-system is still in high degree a recourse to conjecture. Conjecture itself, however, can be systematized. We shall propose some means of such systematizing. *Decision* is choice in face of a lack of sufficient knowledge, and so the study of decision is the study of conjectural appraisal and assessment. The *investment decision*, the choice of the character, scale and timing of durable productive facilities to be acquired, necessarily shares this character of the *management of uncertainty*. This is what we have to study in this chapter. Besides uncertainty, however, the investment decision must allow for the deferment of the gains which it pursues. The operation of discounting, the means of making this allowance, offers also a means of allowing for uncertainty. We shall accordingly begin Section 2 of this chapter with a formal description of the dis-

77

counting operation and show its application and consequences for the investment-decision.

Durability seems at the outset a very simple element in the character of a tool. Yet all the complexities of investment centre on it. If the values of the services that a tool may be able to render in the distant future are highly uncertain and unknowable, why trouble to make tools durable? Why go in for durability, when it is no more than a road lost in the abyss of time? Why not use non-durable tools? The reason lies, we may fairly say, in the nature of physical things, in the unarguable facts of technology. A tool can be built with near-miraculous powers, effecting huge economies of human effort or doing what no number of men without its aid could ever do; fabricating, shaping or assembling with humanly incomparable precision, force and speed; computing beyond anything the human brain can compass in a lifetime; condensing and concentrating vast energies into infinitesimal spaces and moments of time. But such a tool is so expensive to make, that if it could only be used on a single occasion, or only for a day or a week, even such transcendent capabilities could not enable it to earn its first cost. Durability gives us the *only hope* that the most expensive tools can pay for themselves. To say that the prospect of their paying for themselves depends on a conjectural future (which is true) is simply to say that we either accept this uncertainty or totally renounce the help of such tools. Thus, then, the problem of fitting an act of investment into a policy which can commend itself, is the problem of finding for such acts a frame of thought which can relate them to the visible outlines of a firm's circumstances.

2. DISCOUNTING

A *principal* is a sum of P money units handed today by a lender to a borrower in exchange for the latter's promise to make payments of stated numbers of money units on stated future dates. The *deferment* of any such promised payment is the number N of time-units (say years) separating today from the due date of payment. If there is only one such promised payment, the making of which will complete and round off the entire transaction of lending and repayment, this single payment may be called the *amount*, A, to which the borrower's debt will have risen by the due date of its payment. For a reason which we shall immediately examine, the amount will exceed the principal. If the amount is due to be paid one year from today's handing over of the principal, the difference $A - P = rP$ may be called the *interest per annum*, and r, a proper fraction such as $1/20$, $1/30$, or $1/12$, commonly expressed as a percentage, is the *rate of interest per annum*. Thus we have

$$A = P + rP = P(1 + r)$$

and so, dividing both sides by $(1 + r)$,

$$P = A/(1 + r)$$

Suppose now that the borrower's single payment is to be made two years from today. Then *one* year hence, the borrower will owe $P(1 + r)$, and if instead of then paying that amount he waits a further year, he will in effect be borrowing, for that second year, not P but $P(1 + r)$. What will be the amount at the end of the second year? If $P(1 + r)$ is lent for a year at an annual interest rate of r, its amount after that year will be

$$P(1 + r) + rP(1 + r) = P(1 + r)(1 + r) = P(1 + r)^2$$

If the debt is to run on for N years at an interest rate of r per annum, its eventual amount will be $P(1 + r)^N$. A debt which runs on from year to year, having the interest due at each year-end added to it at that date, is said to *accumulate at compound interest*. Instead of calculating the amount A of a principal P accumulated at compound interest of r per annum for N years, we can calculate the present value, P, of a payment of known amount, A money units, deferred N years (due in N years from now). This is done by solving the equation

$$A = P(1 + r)^N$$

for P, by dividing both sides by $(1 + r)^N$, so that

$$P = A/(1 + r)^N$$

We have thus *discounted* the amount A at an interest rate of r per annum for a deferment of N years. If r is unknown, we evidently require numerical values for A, P and N in order to assign a numerical value to r.

Why should it be necessary for borrowers to pay, and possible for lenders to exact, an interest rate? The borrower's promise to make stated payments at stated dates, called a *bond*, is an asset which can be sold by the lender to a third party. A market exists for the sale of bonds, and this bond market is a section of the Stock Exchange. The original act of borrowing can itself be regarded as the sale of a bond by the borrower in the open market, that is to say, to any one of many competing bidders with money which they wish to lend. The purchaser of such a bond is under no obligation to keep possession of it until all the promised payments shall have been made by the lender. He can himself sell the bond in the open bond-market at any time. How much will he get for it? It is because this question *cannot be answered in advance* that a positive rate of interest prevails.

For we then have two propositions about the lender's situation. He cannot tell, at the moment of lending, that is, at the moment of purchasing a bond old or new, what sum of money he will get for his bond at any future date. And he cannot, at the moment when he buys a bond, tell whether and when he may wish to sell it again and so recover such money as the market at that unknown future date will give for it. The effect of these two propositions, taken together, is that the act of lending is the *exchange of a known for an unknown sum of money*. In order that such a transaction may be acceptable to a lender, the borrower's promised payments due in the future must come to a total larger than the price which the lender has to pay for the bond. For by this means the lender will both be given an odds-on chance of getting his money back, and since there is some chance of his getting more than his money back, he will be compensated by this hope for the discomfort of uncertainty. If, then, the lender pays a price P for a bond which promises payments of $A_1, A_2, \ldots, A_N$ at deferments of 1, 2, $\ldots$, N years, these payments must be such as to satisfy a relation

$$P = \frac{A_1}{1+r} + \frac{A_2}{(1+r)^2} + \cdots + \frac{A_N}{(1+r)^N}$$

where, if the A's were simply added together without being divided by a number larger than unity, they would come to a total greater than P. Being so divided, or *discounted*, they can be made, by a suitable choice of r, to come to a total equal to P. The formula above can be more compactly written by means of the operator-symbol Σ, the Greek capital letter *sigma*, which indicates that all terms of a certain type, within a stated range, are to be added together:

$$P = \sum_{i=1}^{N} A_i/(1+r)^i$$

or

$$P = \sum_{i=1}^{N} A_i(1+r)^{-i}$$

This formula shows that the terms to be included in the addition run from the first year to the Nth, and in its second version, uses a *negative exponent*, $-i$, to indicate *division* by $(1+r)$.

The existence of a bond market, where rates of interest are established by the competitive bidding of would-be borrowers for loans and of would-be lenders for bonds, is for the businessman as much an objective item of his circumstances as is the existence of his product market or his factor markets, where conditions, such as the tastes and knowledge of potential buyers of his product or suppliers of productive services, govern his decisions concerning the size or price of his output. The bond market decrees that a given sum of spot cash available today (whatever proper name, such as August 16, 1970, may identify 'today') can be exchanged today for some other larger, named sum guaranteed by some borrower to be available at some named future date. Any transaction which the businessman is proposing to undertake, whether of buying and selling goods or of productive activity, whose financial consequences amount to the exchange of money now for money then, will take care that his exchange is not less favourable to him than the one he could effect by buying a bond. Any packet of trading revenue which his contemplated productive activity, or his contemplated investment in productive facilities, seems to offer him must therefore be *discounted* from its own date to the present, in order that it may be validly compared with the expense, reckoned as made today, which will be the price of having that packet of revenue in prospect.

3. PLANT ACCOUNTING

A system or item of durable productive facilities (a plant) can be conveniently looked on, for the purpose of analysing the decision whether to acquire it, as the source of a firm's output of saleable products. Other inputs, besides the services of the plant itself, will of course be needed: materials and human services of many kinds. The expense ascribable to any dated (proper-named) interval on account of such inputs will be properly reckoned by multiplying the quantities applied in the interval by the prices for such kinds of input assumed to prevail in the interval. The output of the interval will be similarly valued by multiplying its quantity by the price per unit which the product is assumed to fetch in the interval. When for some dated interval, the expense for inputs other than the services of the plant itself is subtracted from the value of the output, the result is the plant's trading revenue for the interval. Let us suppose that the businessman assigns to each future year some one number (in general, a different number for each year) as the plant's assumed trading revenue for that year. Then his valuation of the plant will be the sum of the answers obtained, when each such number has been discounted at the interest rate prevailing in the bond market 'today' for the deferment appropriate to the particular packet of trading revenue. If, then, $Q_1, Q_2, \ldots, Q_N$ stand respectively for the assumed packets of trading revenue ascribed to the end of year 1, year 2, up to year N from today, the businessman's valuation v of his contemplated plant will be

$$v = \frac{Q_1}{1+r} + \frac{Q_2}{(1+r)^2} + \cdots + \frac{Q_N}{(1+r)^N}$$

81

and it is plain that, for any *given* series of Q's, v will be a function of r. It will be a *decreasing* function of r. For the larger is r, the larger will be $1+r$, the smaller will be $1/(1+r) = (1+r)^{-1}$, the smaller will be $(1+r)^{-i}$, and the smaller will be $Q_i (1+r)^{-i}$. Now the questions arise: How powerful, in various circumstances, will be the effect on v of a change in r? What circumstances in particular will affect this leverage? How much will a change in v affect the number of instruments or plants of the type in question which, in any named interval, businessmen all taken together will decide to acquire? And lastly, and of prime and more immediate concern to us, how can the leverage of r on v best be expressed and measured?

4. THE CONCEPT OF ELASTICITY

Elasticity is the proportionate change in a dependent variable divided by the corresponding proportionate change in a variable on which the former depends. We have just seen that the value which a business-man ascribes to some item or system of equipment is a function of the market rate, or rates, of interest by means of which deferred packets of revenue are to be expressed in terms of spot-cash. In saying that the value of the equipment at some 'today' depends on the market interest rates prevailing on this day, we are of course not saying that it depends *only* on these. Plainly this value depends not only on the rate of interest at which assumed future revenue-packets are discounted, but also on the size of these packets themselves. But given those sizes, we can treat the value v of an equipment item as a function of the interest rate r. Thus we can calculate an elasticity of equipment-value with respect to interest. This expression is of concern to us, since it allows us to see under what conditions the value of a contemplated purchase of equipment will be substantially affected by a change in the interest rate, and exactly what characteristics of a series of deferred revenue-packets render the value of this series sensitive to such an interest-rate change. Because of the manifold (indeed, more than infinitely numerous) *time-shapes* which such a series of expected or assumed future packets of trading revenue can in general take, we shall not be able to find any simple or useful general expression for the elasticity of the value of such a series with respect to interest. Instead, we shall show some principles which govern the outcome and some representative cases.

5. DEFERMENT AND THE LEVERAGE OF INTEREST-RATE CHANGES

The expected trading revenues from a plant need not be thought of as divided into annual packets. Every moment of the relevant future, every moment no matter of how short a duration, can be deemed to have its own packet of trading revenue, whose size in relation to the length of that moment will constitute a *speed of flow* of trading revenue into the firm's cash resources. That speed of flow can itself be thought of as a variable depending on the distance of the particular moment in question from the present, that is, upon its *futurity*. Let us then write.

u for the number of money-units per time unit of trading revenue occurring at some moment

x for the futurity of that moment

$u = u(x)$ for the function connecting speed of flow with futurity.

Just as we discounted annual packets we must discount momentary packets of trading revenue at the interest rate prevailing 'today' for loans whose debt is to accumulate from today until the date of the packet. However, there is a more convenient way of expressing this relation of present value to face value of a deferred sum than the one we used previously. The infinite series

$$\frac{1}{0!} + \frac{1}{1!} + \frac{1}{2!} + \frac{1}{3!} + \ldots$$

where the symbol 3! (factorial three) means the product $1 \times 2 \times 3$ of all the natural numbers up to three, and in general $n!$ means $1 \times 2 \times 3 \times \ldots \times n$, and where 0! is defined as unity, has a numerical value usually approximated 2·71828, though it is really an infinite non-recurring decimal. This number, always written e, has peculiar properties which make it specially convenient as the base of natural (Naperian) logarithms. We shall use the Greek letter ρ (rho) for the natural logarithm of the factor $(1+r)$ by which we multiplied the principal of a loan to find its amount after one year:

$$\rho = \log_e(1+r)$$

It so happens that for the ordinarily occurring interest rates up to, say, 10 per cent per annum, ρ has a numerical value rather close to that of r, and, of course, increasing as r increases, so that, for example, $\log_e 1·06 \simeq 0·0583$ and $\log_e 1·10 \simeq 0·0953$, and we shall speak of ρ as the interest rate. It would, indeed, be better to base our explanation of the conceptions of accumulation at compound interest, and of discounting at compound interest, on the notion of *continuous* compounding. The most natural and fundamental idea is that of a mode of growth in which each momentary increment itself begins to grow, at the same proportionate speed as the existing accumulated stock, at the very instant when it is added to that stock, so that at every instant or in every moment the *whole* existing stock is growing at the given proportion of itself per unit of time. If r is a speed of proportionate growth expressed in terms of annual compounding, so that the stock changes abruptly from a size Q to a size $Q(1+r)$ after the lapse of a year, then $\rho = \log_e (1+r)$ is the same speed of growth expressed in terms of continuous, moment-by-moment, compounding. Now we can write the present value, or discounted value, z, of a packet of trading revenue u deferred one year, as

$$z = ue^{-\rho} \tag{4.1}$$

for this is the same as writing $z = u (1+r)^{-1}$ or $z = u/(1+r)$. If u is deferred x years, or time-units, instead of only one year, we have $z = ue^{-\rho x}$. This expression evidently depends on both the interest rate, ρ, and the deferment, x, and we are free to seek its partial derivative with respect to either of these variables.

Let us first consider what happens to z when ρ changes by a small difference, supposing that x meanwhile remains unchanged. If z takes a numerical value z_1 when ρ takes a numerical value ρ_1, and if similarly z_2 corresponds to ρ_2, the ratio $(z_2-z_1)/(\rho_2-\rho_1)$ is a difference-quotient which takes a succession of generally distinct values as we select ρ_2 nearer and nearer to ρ_1. This succession of values is said to tend to a limit which is called the (partial) derivative of z with respect to ρ. The partial derivative expresses the rate of change of one variable with respect to the other *at a point* (ρ_1, z_1). We have as the expression of this partial derivative

$$\frac{\partial z}{\partial \rho} = -uxe^{-\rho x} \tag{4.2}$$

and this expression is itself a function of both ρ and x, so that the answer to the question how much does z change when ρ changes by a given small amount depends on both the interest rate and the deferment. If ρ is given, that answer depends on x, and we can differentiate the identity (4.2) with respect to deferment x. The resulting expression will show how the leverage of the interest rate on the present value of a deferred sum is affected by the length of that deferment. We have

$$\frac{\partial}{\partial x}\left(\frac{\partial z}{\partial \rho}\right) = (\rho x - 1)ue^{-\rho x} \tag{4.3}$$

Will the leverage be greatest at some particular deferment or futurity? We know that if so, it will be when the expression (4.3) is equal to zero. Solving the equation

$$(\rho x - 1)ue^{-\rho x} = 0$$

84

we have as one solution

$$\rho x - 1 = 0$$

or

$$x = \frac{1}{\rho} \qquad (4.4)$$

The only other way of making $(\rho x - 1)ue^{-\rho x}$ approach zero would be to let x tend to infinity, since this would make the factor $e^{-\rho x}$, or $1/e^{\rho x}$, tend to zero. The businessman is not interested in infinity, and so for him the greatest leverage of interest-rate changes is exerted on that packet of trading revenue whose deferment, expressed as a number of years, is equal to the *reciprocal* of the annual interest rate.

x	$\dfrac{\partial z}{\partial \rho}$	x	$\dfrac{\partial z}{\partial \rho}$	x	$\dfrac{\partial z}{\partial \rho}$	x	$\dfrac{\partial z}{\partial \rho}$
0	0	15	−9·56	30	−12·20	45	−11·67
1	−0·97	16	−9·90	31	−12·23	46	−11·57
2	−1·88	17	−10·20	32	−12·25	47	−11·47
3	−2·73	18	−10·49	33	−12·26	48	−11·37
4	−3·55	19	−10·74	34	−12·26	49	−11·27
5	−4·30	20	−10·98	35	−12·25	50	−11·16
6	−5·00	21	−11·18	36	−12·22	51	−11·04
7	−5·67	22	−11·37	37	−12·19	52	−10·93
8	−6·29	23	−11·54	38	−12·15	53	−10·81
9	−6·87	24	−11·68	39	−12·10	54	−10·69
10	−7·41	25	−11·81	40	−12·05	55	−10·56
11	−7·91	26	−11·92	41	−11·98	56	−10·44
12	−8·37	27	−12·01	42	−11·91	57	−10·31
13	−8·80	28	−12·09	43	−11·83	58	−10·18
14	−9·20	29	−12·15	44	−11·75	59	−10·00
						60	− 9·92

TABLE 4.1

$$\frac{\partial z}{\partial \rho} = -xue^{-\rho x}$$

with $\rho = 0{\cdot}03$, $u = 1$

Table 4.1 shows the numerical values of the partial derivative of z with respect to ρ for deferments from zero up to 60 years, for $\rho = 0{\cdot}03$ and $u = 1$. These values are the means of drawing a continuous curve of $\partial z/\partial \rho = -xe^{-\rho x}$ shown in Fig. 4.1. Our preceding analysis has led us to expect that changes of the interest rate will have their

85

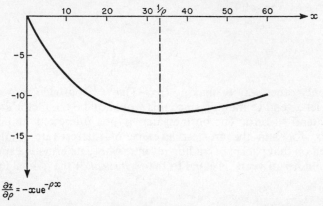

Graph of $\partial z/\partial \rho = -xue^{-\rho x}$ with $u = 1$, $\rho = 0.03$. When $z = ue^{-\rho x}$, $\partial z/\partial \rho$ has a minimum at $x = 1/\rho$.

FIG. 4.1

greatest absolute (not proportionate) effect on the present value of a given packet of trading revenue, when that packet is deferred by a number of years equal to the reciprocal of the interest rate; that is, in our illustrative case, $33\frac{1}{3}$ years. In Fig. 4.1, we see the effect of a change of the interest rate increasing steeply as we move out through near future years, reaching a numerical maximum (algebraically a minimum, since $\partial z/\partial \rho$ takes negative values everywhere) at $33\frac{1}{3}$ years and thereafter decreasing as the absolute shrinkage of present values overcomes to an increasing degree the ever-increasing *proportional* reduction of each such value by its multiplication by an ever-smaller factor $e^{-\rho x}$. The segment of $\partial z/\partial \rho$ shown in Fig. 4.1 terminates at about that deferment where it has a *point of inflexion*, that is to say, where its approach to the axis of x ceases to get steeper and begins to get flatter. The curve can never attain the axis of x, since the expression $-xe^{-\rho x}$ never becomes zero at any finite value of x.

The effect of increasing deferment in at first increasing and then decreasing the absolute effect of an interest-rate change on the present value of a given packet of trading revenue is shown in an alternative way in Fig. 4.2. Here we plot the present values themselves, $z = ue^{-\rho x}$, for $u = 1$ and for $\rho = 0.03$ and $\rho = 0.05$ respectively. The 'northward' distance between the two curves at first increases as we move 'eastward' to greater and greater deferments, then decreases again, as the more southerly curve, for $\rho = 0.05$, finds itself in an ever-shrinking gap between the more northerly curve and the deferment axis. Within this shrinking gap, the curve for $\rho = 0.05$ lies nearer and nearer the deferment axis, showing how,

86

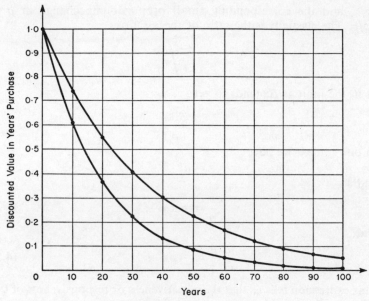

Upper curve: $\rho = 0.03$
Lower curve: $\rho = 0.05$

FIG. 4.2

though a given change of the interest rate makes a larger and larger proportionate change in z, this proportion affects a smaller and smaller z, so that the absolute change gets smaller with increasing deferment.

6. THE INTEREST ELASTICITY OF PRESENT VALUES

In the symbol for a difference-quotient, say $\Delta z/\Delta\rho$, or its value in the limit as $\Delta\rho$ tends to zero, written $\partial z/\partial\rho$, we are of course thinking of two corresponding differences. We take two values z_1 and ρ_1 which are paired together by some function, and two other values z_2 and ρ_2 which are similarly associated by the function, and form the ratio $(z_2 - z_1)/(\rho_2 - \rho_1)$ from which we proceed to the limiting value $\partial z/\partial\rho$ by supposing $\rho_2 - \rho_1$ to tend to zero while z_2 and z_1 take those values which the function dictates according to the changes of ρ_2 and ρ_1. However, it is allowable to manipulate such a symbol as Δz without keeping it in direct relation to its corresponding difference $\Delta\rho$, and to obtain a formal notation for the idea of elasticity. Thus a 'small proportionate change in z' becomes

$\Delta z/z$, and the corresponding small proportionate change in ρ is $\Delta\rho/\rho$. The elasticity is the ratio of these ratios,

$$\eta = \frac{\Delta z}{z} \bigg/ \frac{\Delta\rho}{\rho}$$

or in the limit as Δz tends to zero

$$\eta = \frac{\partial z}{\partial \rho} \frac{\rho}{z}$$

In our context we have

$$z = ue^{-\rho x}$$

and so

$$\frac{\partial z}{\partial \rho} = -xue^{-\rho x}$$

and

$$\frac{\partial z}{\partial \rho} \frac{\rho}{z} = -\rho x \qquad (4.5)$$

This expression tells us that the sensitiveness or responsiveness of the present value of a deferred packet of trading revenue to changes in the interest rate used for discounting it, increases in (negative) numerical value in direct proportion to its deferment and to the interest rate itself. From this fact alone we can broadly infer the effect of the time-shape of a stream of expected trading revenues on its present value. If this stream comprises large packets of revenue in the near future and none, or only small ones, in more distant years, the leverage of interest will be small. If the early years seem bound to be barren while the trading revenues are assumed to mount up in more distant ones, the leverage of interest will be great. But in applying this broad notion we must have regard to what we saw in Section 5. The increasing *elasticities* which apply to remote future years have their absolute effect reduced by the very power of compound interest itself, which means that the present values of those long-deferred packets of trading revenue, in which present values a given change in interest can effect so great a *proportionate* change, are comparatively small, so that this large proportionate change has only a small *weighting* in the calculation of the elasticity, with respect to the interest rate, of the present value of the entire stream of expected trading revenues as a whole.

Now let us turn from consideration of individual packets of discounted trading revenue to that of their sum, which constitutes the value of the plant from which these trading revenues are assumed to be derived. This sum will be written

$$v = \int_o^L ue^{-\rho x} dx$$

where the integral sign $\int$, a medieval long s, is an operator instructing us to add together all such elements or 'packets' as $ue^{-\rho x}dx$ (each of which can be pictured as a strip of a height $ue^{-\rho x}$ and a width dx) which come within the range of x from $x = 0$ (the businessman's present moment) to $x = L$, the most distant date at which it is assumed that any revenue will be drawn from the plant, whether by way of operating results or scrap value. In writing the above expression for v we have put the symbol u, standing for undiscounted packets of trading revenue, inside the expression covered by (following) the integral sign. This position is appropriate if we regard u as essentially a variable depending on x. But if we treat u as a constant independent of x, so that all undiscounted packets of trading revenue are assumed to be equal, we can write u outside the integral itself, as a coefficient. In this case by performing the integration we have

$$v = u \int_o^L e^{-\rho x} dx = \frac{u}{\rho}(1 - e^{-\rho L}) \tag{4.6}$$

If u is an arbitrary constant, we can simplify matters by putting it equal to unity (that is to say, choosing our unit of undiscounted trading revenue to be equal to this constant unit-time flow of trading revenue), so as to have

$$v = \frac{1}{\rho}(1 - e^{-\rho L}) \tag{4.7}$$

Now the elasticity η of v with respect to ρ is defined as the proportionate change of v divided by the corresponding proportionate change of ρ, that is to say,

$$\eta = \frac{\partial v}{v} \bigg/ \frac{\partial \rho}{\rho}$$

$$= \frac{\rho}{v} \frac{\partial v}{\partial \rho}$$

Using our expression (4.6) above, we then have for η

$$\frac{\rho}{v} \frac{\partial v}{\partial \rho} = \frac{e^{-\rho L}(1 + \rho L) - 1}{1 - e^{-\rho L}} \tag{4.8}$$

As L tends to infinity, the numerical value of η tends to minus one, since $e^{-\rho L}$ tends to zero. That is to say, when the expected stream of trading revenues stretches out limitlessly far into the future, the response of its present value to, say, an increase of the interest rate by one-hundredth of itself, for example from 5 per cent per annum to 5·05 per cent per annum, will be a fall of the present value by approximately one-hundredth of itself. For finite values of L, η will lie between zero and minus one, so that, for example, at $L = 10$, $\rho = 0.03$ we have $\eta = -0.9$.

Use of the differential calculus entails considering 'small' changes of the independent variable. Indeed we consider an endless succession of terms in each successive term of which the difference of the independent variable is taken smaller than in the preceding term, and we may, if we wish, find the meaning of the derivative in an imaginary process of writing down one more and yet one more such term forever. But we can, of course, dispense with the calculus method and consider the relation to each other of mutually associated 'large' changes of the two variables. It will be convenient here to express the present value of an assumed series or stream of *equal* yearly, daily or momently packets of trading revenue in terms of *years' purchase*. This simply means that we take as our unit of value the number of money units that each year's flow of the stream is assumed to be going to bring in.

Table 4.2 divides the life of a plant, which is assumed to be going to earn equal annual trading revenues for eighty years and thereafter nothing, into decades. Column 1 shows for each decade, in terms of years' purchase, the value of its trading revenues discounted to the present (the beginning of the eighty-year life) at an interest rate of 4 per cent per annum. Column 2 shows the same at 2 per cent per annum. Column 3 shows what percentage of the plant's total value is attributable to each decade, when its assumed trading revenues over the eighty years are discounted at 4 per cent, and column 4 shows the same for 2 per cent. Column 5 shows the excess of each entry in column 2 over the corresponding entry in column 1. Column 6 shows what percentage of the total *gain* of value, arising from the change of interest rate from 4 per cent to 2 per cent, is ascribable to each decade. The implications of this table reinforce and illustrate our analytical conclusions. We see that at 4 per cent per annum, more than one-third of the plant's total present value is ascribable to the first of its assumed eight decades. Even at 2 per cent (an impractically low rate even when the possibility of inflation is ignored by the public) nearly seven-tenths arises from the first half of the plant's life. When the plant has an eighty-year assumed life, the halving of the interest rate increases the present value by 16/24ths. If it was assumed to be going to earn constant annual trading revenues for only forty years, the gain of present value from this halving of the interest rate would be only 9/24ths. The gain of value ascribable to each decade rises to a

TABLE 4.2

Decade	Present value, in terms of trading years' purchase, of trading revenue in each decade		Percentage of total value of plant attributable to the trading revenue of each decade		Excess of column (2) over column 1	Percentage of total gain in value attributable to each decade
	$\rho = 0.04$ 1	$\rho = 0.02$ 2	$\rho = 0.04$ 3	$\rho = 0.02$ 4	5	6
1	8·24	9·06	34·5	22·6	0·82	5·0
2	5·52	7·42	23·2	18·7	1·90	12·0
3	3·70	6·07	15·4	15·3	2·37	15·0
4	2·48	4·97	10·3	12·5	2·49	15·7
5	1·68	4·07	7·1	10·2	2·39	15·0
6	1·12	3·33	4·8	8·3	2·21	14·0
7	0·75	2·73	3·2	6·8	1·98	12·5
8	0·50	2·23	2·1	5·6	1·73	11·0
Total	24·00 (approx.)	40·00 (approx.)	100·0	100·0	16·00 (approx.)	100·0

maximum in the fourth decade and then falls again. Its apparent lateness, in comparison with our analytical finding that the greatest absolute effect on present value occurs at a futurity equal to the reciprocal of the interest rate, is due to the size of the change in interest that we have assumed in Table 4.2 in contrast with the incipient or 'marginal' changes supposed in our analysis. The most important implication of the table, however, is the great length of prospective earning life which is needed in order to give changes of the interest rate any considerable leverage. Using assumptions at the opposite extreme we find for instance that, if the plant were assigned only a five-year life of constant annual trading revenues, its present value would be increased, by a fall of interest from 4 per cent to 3 per cent, by only one-fortieth, while with a ten-year life the same reduction of interest by one percentage point would increase the present value by less than one-twentieth.

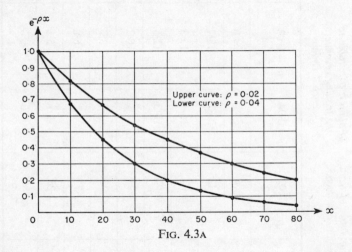

FIG. 4.3A

Table 4.2 is pictured in Fig. 4.3A. Here, on the east–west axis, zero stands for 'the present', the businessman's viewpoint in time. The ordinates of each curve, its northward distances from the east–west axis, show the effect of discounting the expected trading revenues, assumed to be going to flow at an even and continuous pace, over their respective time-distances from the present, at $\rho = 0.04$ or $\rho = 0.02$ respectively. Each entry in column 1 or column 2 of Table 4.2 is represented by the area enclosed under the curve between that pair of ordinates which mark the beginning and the end of the decade in question. Similar curves for $\rho = 0.06$ and $\rho = 0.03$ are shown in Fig. 4.3B.

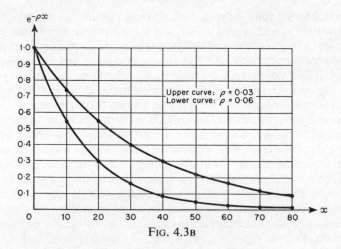

FIG. 4.3B

We have examined in some depth the effect which changes of the interest rate can in principle exert on the values which businessmen set on plant and equipment-systems which they might acquire. This is, of course, only one link in a chain of influences leading from the interest rate to the size of flow of industrial investment in society as a whole. We have examined this link first, not because it is quantitatively the most dominant, but because it leads to the more conventional of two ways of treating a more powerful influence, namely the conjectural nature of expected trading revenues.

7. THE RESERVOIR OF INVESTMENT PROJECTS

The account which used to be given of a society's mode of building up its general system or stock of industrial equipment stands in strong contrast to the one we are presenting. That earlier view, conforming in basic assumptions to the continental (as opposed to the Marshallian) scheme of the determination of relative values which was constructed in the later nineteenth century, rested on the supposition that men's economic conduct springs from the fully informed and perfectly logical pursuit of their interests. In order to be fully informed, however, men must be emancipated from time. There must be no possibility of new insights and inventions. So long as there can be novelty, knowledge is not complete. Thus the so-called neo-classical theory of relative values applied only to a timeless world, and the notion of a process of building up equipment was logically quite alien to it. Yet of course such a process is central to our way of life and it must be studied. It is the idea that men are, or can conceivably be, fully informed of all their circumstances, which we must wholly abandon and reject. Let us summarize briefly an argument we have already traced. First, a man's circumstances essentially include the concurrent and the future decisions and intentions of others. Their concurrent decisions and intentions, which they are evolving or entertaining at the same moment as he is forming his own, can perhaps in some measure be known through their incipient effect on the market. But if the word *decision* means what, in ordinary speech and thought, we use it for, a decision is by its essential nature incapable of being known in advance. Decisions are formed or taken at particular moments. To know, before such a moment is reached, what one will then decide is a contradiction in terms, a logical absurdity. If the meaning we give to decision in everyday, instinctive and unselfconscious usage has any referend in reality, then part of a man's or firm's circumstances is essentially unknowable. But a more mundane fact is equally compelling. Business life is full of the endeavours of men and firms to conceal their real intentions and even to give misleading evidence about them. Thus the process of bargaining centrally involves the endeavour of each party to conceal from the other the constraints which his own true desires and circumstances impose upon his own action. In such cases of bilateral monopoly, as also in duopoly, namely the rivalry of two firms in an isolated market, the main weapon of each side is concealment and deception. Secrecy and deliberate misguidance are as much a part of business as of war. And finally, there is novelty. In a world where nothing is more continually discussed or more ardently and expensively pursued than technological innovation, the fact of a vast and perhaps illimitable area of yet-to-be-discovered knowledge is taken for granted. The whole spirit of business is to out-do one's rivals by inventing or adopting a new technique or a new product and exploiting its potentiality during some interval before it can be imitated. The old view of the investment process, in the hands of some continental writers, totally neglected innovation and, in effect, assumed that investment would only occur when a gradual sinking of the interest rate, which they thought would be brought about by the steady process of saving, had sufficiently raised the value of some kind of equipment to bring this value above the supply price or construction-cost of that equipment. The social process thus envisaged may be compared to the withdrawal of the tide which gradually exposes more and more of the shoals and sandbanks. This was never the view of Alfred Marshall. Though his life and work were contemporary with those of the builders of the general equilibrium system, and of those of the writers who tacked on to it an account of the process and effect of saving, he was, by contrast, very largely concerned with what he looked upon as the inevitable discovery of ever more economical methods of production. Methods of production, and the equipment embodying them, which have remained unadopted because the interest rate has not fallen low enough, are perhaps unlikely ever to be adopted, because they will be superseded. Nonetheless, we shall do well to devise a formal picture of a situation where a dramatic fall of the interest rate seems possible and where, perhaps, many businessmen, having in mind desirable extensions of their equipment, are waiting for this fall to happen so as to finance these extensions economically.

At any historical moment each member of some list of businessmen will have in mind a design of plant which he has evolved in view of his own circumstances and on which he is ready to set a value summarizing his judgement of its promise and potentialities. We may suppose that value to express his mind in the sense that if it exceeds the lowest price which a contractor will tender for the plant, he will order it. The contingent investment plans to be found in the list of businessmen at the particular moment will vary enormously in scale, and we must allow for this by adopting a unit of investment of, say, 1 million pounds, and treating a 10-million pound plant as composed of ten plants of unit size each represented by its own symbol on our diagram. In Fig. 4.4 the top (or 'northernmost') horizontal line

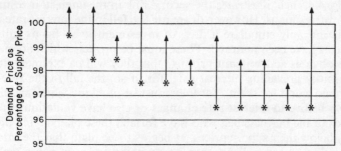

Effect on valuations of investment projects of a fall of the interest rate by one percentage point

FIG. 4.4

represents the supply price (lowest price tendered by any contractor) for a unit plant. This is the 100 per cent line. The ladder of horizontal lines below this represent 99 per cent, 98 per cent, and so on of the supply price for a unit plant. Each star in the diagram represents by its north–south position the businessman's valuation or 'demand price' for a plant of a particular design. The arrow extending northwards from each such star represents by its length the degree to which a fall of one percentage point in the interest rate, from its level prevailing at the historical moment in question, would raise the value of the plant. The lengths of these arrows can greatly differ, because the effect of a given fall of interest rates upon the value of a series of deferred trading revenues depends, as we have seen, on their distribution over future time.

It is plain that the situation represented in any such diagram is the outcome of events over many past years. If the interest rate has recently risen from much lower levels, after standing at those lower levels for some years, and if, in the short time since that rise, invention and innovation have not been active, or if that time has been too short for plans based on those recent technological advances to have been fully developed and a value set on them, there may be a blank zone containing few or no projects whose value would be lifted to the supply price, or above it, by a fall of the rate of interest by one percentage point. But if the rate has reached its present level by a steady secular decline, as envisaged by those writers who made the interest rate to depend on the technical and physical productivity of existing equipment and supposed it to fall as this equipment was accumulated, then a one percentage point further fall is evidently likely to bring to the level of viability a great many projects embodying long-available technology which it has not hitherto paid to exploit.

Fig. 4.4, then, illustrates the second link in the interest–investment train of reactions. However dramatic the fall in the interest rate may be, it can only stimulate a flow of investment in so far as suitable projects have been matured. These must be projects which are not of such obvious and brilliant promise that they will be exploited at the previously prevailing interest rate, for, if so, the fall in the rate can claim no credit for them. Yet they must be of a kind which are either very sensitive to interest-rate changes or else have valuations (in the minds of the businessmen who have formed these plans) lying only a little below their supply prices. It begins to be plain that the interest rate will need a world of rather steady-going and even-paced technological advance, and a world stable enough to give small differences of value a meaning and influence, if it is to exert much control over the flow of investment. And that control will be mainly on those kinds of equipment which promise a very long and secure economic life, pre-eminently such investments as houses.

Even when the degrees of responsiveness of present values to changes of the interest rate, for those types of investment-project which have actually, at the moment in question, been brought to a stage of readiness for execution, and further, the distribution of values of such ready projects in relation to their supply price, have been

96

taken into account, there is still one more link in the chain of reactions leading from interest to investment. This third link is the *supply-conditions* of investment-goods of the types likely to be demanded. For the concept of elasticity applies to supply as well as demand. How much will the supply prices, at which contractors tender for the construction of plants, be pushed up by a given increase in the quantity of such plants for which tenders are invited? If the construction and plant-making industries are working near to capacity, any increase of orders *must* result either in a raising of tendered prices so that some of the potential demand is discouraged, or else in a lengthening of promised delivery or completion dates, which in itself is a cost, since it increases the deferment of hoped for trading revenues and reduces their present value.

8. UNCERTAINTY, DISCOUNTING AND HORIZON

Expensive tools, we saw, need much time in which to repay their first cost. That time must needs lie in a future which is out of reach of direct observation, which in strictness is *unknowable*. How can the businessman build reason upon ignorance? What frame of thought will enable him ever to say to himself that some given act of investment is worth while? There are two highly contrasted approaches to this problem. One of them asks what bounds a man can put to his ignorance, the other asks what qualifications he must admit to his knowledge. The former is exemplified by the scheme of focus values which we shall describe in Chapter 5 where a man asks himself what is the worst that can happen to his fortune as a consequence of a given proposed act of investment, and whether his exposure to this injury is overcome, in the scales of his own emotions, by a sufficiently dazzling possibility of success. What do we mean by *possibility*? The possibility of some outcome is of course a human judgement, a characteristic of thought and not of Nature. But the decision to invest requires men, and not Nature, to be satisfied. Nature's power in the matter is limited to retribution and does not extend to veto. In judging what is possible and what is tolerable, the businessman is guided by what we shall call his *practical conscience*, his instinct for avoiding those acts which seem to endanger his firm's survival. The second way in which he may satisfy this instinct is to form a single 'best guess' as to what the outcome of the investment may be, and then reduce its value to allow for its quality of guesswork. We may say that in this approach he *discounts* his assumed trading revenues for uncertainty.

Discounting, as a means of legislating for uncertainty, has considerable practical merits. Such light as is thrown on the future, by a

G 97

knowledge of the present, dims rapidly as the vista deepens into remote years. An arithmetical procedure formally identical with that which allows for deferment will have an increasingly powerful effect on increasingly remote assumed revenues. Yet this effect is not perfectly adapted to the needs of the matter. There is market evidence, as well as introspective suggestion, for the view that effective ignorance of future business conditions does not worsen indefinitely as we look further ahead, but gets as bad as it can be at about ten years' futurity, at which distance nothing worth while can be said about how things will be. Thus discounting for uncertainty should use a percentage per annum which will reduce almost to nothing the present value of any revenues lying beyond ten years ahead. This effect ought ideally to increase steeply in power over the early years and then approach more and more gradually its total obliteration of present values. In arithmetical fact it may not precisely match this required pattern but it approximates it for practical purposes.

In Chapter 1 we referred to the notion of *horizon*, the businessman's resolve to allow only those conjectured circumstances and events, which he locates within some specified futurity, to affect his present decisions. His investment-horizon will be that time-distance into the future beyond which all trading revenues from a plant which he might now acquire will be assumed to be zero. If he imposes such a horizon, no investment-project will be acceptable unless the trading revenues which it promises within the horizon are such that their value, when they are discounted at the market interest rates prevailing at the moment of decision, is at least equal to the cost of acquisition of the plant. The time-distance of the horizon can then be called the project's *pay-off period*. The concept of horizon has its peculiar subtlety. Its meaning is of course the recognition that the more distant the date considered, the more worthless are any conjectures as to what situation may then prevail. As the horizon is brought nearer to the present, the larger must be the annual trading revenues which a project of given cost must offer in order to be acceptable. Thus the more striking and implausible will appear the contrast between these larger supposed revenues in the years up to the horizon, and the zero revenues thereafter. The nearness of the horizon thus provides a safety-net for the conjectures of trading revenue. If the larger revenues of near-future years seem genuinely possible, it is permissible for the businessman to entertain some hopes of further positive revenues beyond those early years. To bring the horizon nearer thus offers a double safeguard against disappointment. It implies a main reliance only on the near and fairly 'visible' future, the future which is conjecturable by the assumption that change is limited in speed and that recent tendencies have some momentum.

And secondly, it offers some presumption that revenues will continue beyond the horizon, and tend to make up for any deficiencies and disappointment from those before it.

Let us turn back to the idea of discounting for uncertainty. If the businessman uses for this purpose a percentage per annum, that percentage can simply be added to the market rate of interest to form a combined discount rate which will allow for both deferment and uncertainty and provide a demand price suitable to be directly compared with the supply price. Table 4.3 shows the present value, in

TABLE 4.3

5-year period	Present value, in terms of years' purchase, of trading revenue in each five-year period		Percentage of total value of plant attributable to the trading revenue of each five-year period	
	discounted at 33% per annum	discounted at 18% per annum	discounted at 33% per annum	discounted at 18% per annum
1	2·424	3·294	80·8	61·0
2	0·466	1·339	15·6	24·8
3	0·089	0·544	3·0	10·1
4	0·017	0·221	0·6	4·1
Total	2·996	5·398	100·0	100·0

terms of years' purchase, of the trading revenues in each five-year period of the supposed twenty-year earning life of a plant, during each year of which life its trading revenue is assumed to be the same. The result of discounting these revenues at 33 per cent per annum is shown in column 1 and at 18 per cent in column 2. Column 3 shows the percentage of the plant's total value which is ascribable to each five-year period for discounting at 33 per cent per annum, and column 4 shows the same for discounting at 18 per cent per annum. The ascription of 80 per cent of the value to the first five-year period (column 2) may perhaps be held equivalent to a five-year horizon, and the ascription of 86 per cent to the first two five-year periods, in column 4, is equivalent to a ten-year horizon. Thus we vindicate the claim that discounting for uncertainty, on one hand, and the use of the pay-off period, on the other, are two methods for securing the same effect. When a businessman speaks of requiring a proposed investment to earn, say, 33 per cent on its first cost if it is to be acceptable, we may be in doubt whether he means simply that for a few years its undiscounted trading revenues must be counted on to bear that ratio to the first cost, or whether he is using the more subtle notion of discounting for deferment and uncertainty. But in fact it does not matter: in either case he is expressing his requirement of a very near effective horizon. For if he means undiscounted trading revenues, then at 33 per cent per annum these would repay first cost in a little over three years. If he felt sure that a single plant of the design in question would earn such large annual amounts for many years, the attractiveness of its enormous profitability would surely induce himself, if not others, to build sufficient capacity of this type to bring down the rate to a more natural level. It is the lack of ground for the belief, in his own mind and those of others, in the continuance of high earnings beyond the earliest few years, which protects the prospect of such earnings from being washed away in competition. If, instead, the 33 per cent is a rate of discount, then, as we have seen in Table 4.3, it will reduce to insignificance the earnings beyond those few earliest years.

9. FOCUS VALUES

The two methods we have been discussing by which the businessman can bring uncertainty explicitly into his investment-picture share one basic characteristic. Each of them provides him with a single number as the measure of the value to him of his proposed investment. But such a formulation is not dictated by anything in logic or Nature. It suffers from a distinct disadvantage. For it is of the essence of uncertainty that *plural rival hypotheses* can be entertained concerning some question. And it is of great concern to the businessman whether these rivals are closely similar to each other or widely disparate. A single figure of present value or of required pay-off period can express nothing directly and explicitly of this vital characteristic of his expectations. Why does a businessman contemplate investment? Not in order to secure the guarantee of a modest return on his firm's fortune: that can be done by lending. He is out for large success. By embarking his firm's fortune in plant he puts it in a position where great gains are within its reach, and where it is itself within reach of great misfortunes. Exposure to the best entails exposure to the worst. It can be argued that the businessman's proper task is to find a 'best' whose corresponding 'worst' is not, in contemplation, too high a price to pay. He himself, of course, must judge what best and worst are possible, what worst is tolerable and, in especial, survivable by the firm, and what 'best' is a great enough prize to justify running so near the brink of disaster. In Chapter 5 we shall suggest more precisely what may be involved in this conception of two *focus values* for the outcome of a business enterprise.

The adoption of a single number as the valuation of a contemplated plant can be interpreted in any one of several ways. Two of these correspond very roughly to the statistical concepts of the mode and mean. We may suppose the businessman to ask himself: If I had to bet, at given odds, on one figure only as the outcome of this venture, expressed as its present value, what figure would I name? We may call his answer his 'best guess', and this has some affinity with the mode of a probability distribution. Or we may suppose him to assign probabilities to a variety of outcomes, good and bad, which he writes down. Such probabilities cannot be assigned a statistical meaning in any strict sense. It is not conceivable that plants or enterprises exactly like the one he is contemplating have been ventured on in the past in exactly similar circumstances to his own in any numbers at all, let alone sufficient numbers to serve as a 'sample' of some imaginary universe of such cases. Such an idea is a total denial of the very essence and spirit of modern business, where the constant ambition of each man is to hit upon novelty of product or technique to outdo and render obsolete whatever has been done already. What is *novel* is precisely that about which it is *logically* impossible for any statistical experience to exist. The novel is the *unexperienced*. In Chapters 5 and 7 we shall distinguish between events or situations which are *counter-expected* and those which are *unexpected*. A counter-expected event is the actual occurrence of something the hypothesis of which was earlier examined and in the main rejected as implausible. This judgement can be expressed by assigning to the counter-expected hypothesis a low probability. An unexpected event, however, is the actual occurrence of something quite outside the range and character of all those things which were envisaged. It is the unthought of, the totally disconcerting. We can assign, in advance, a subjective probability to the notion that our list of hypothetical answers to the question 'What will happen?' may prove to have been incomplete, though any basis for such a judgement must be peculiarly elusive. But we cannot assign a probability to any occurrence of a specified nature when the idea of that specified occurrence has never entered our minds. There is a more pressing and practical objection to the use of the notion of average outcome. The individual firm is not a conglomerate of all the firms in its industry or in the notional industry to which this unreal average must be assigned. It is one peculiar and special individual, and to this individual it is not the fate of a phantom host of non-existent other firms which matters, but what can, what may, happen to itself.

In a world where the consequences of deciding to do this or that are essentially and logically beyond the reach of observation and of calculation, where a guaranteed, exact and complete knowledge of them is unattainable, where history exercises in every age and generation her inexhaustible gift of irony and of surprise, no system of prophecy can give objectively sure guidance. We have gone further, and suggested that a great part of business effort is directed to defeating the efforts of one's rivals to know what one is doing and is going to do. Ignorance imposed upon one's enemy is as valuable as knowledge gained for oneself. Knowledge too is paradoxical, for how do we know what was knowledge and what was fallacy until it is too late? Life, action and decision are in the present, the solitary moment of actuality, and decision, which of its nature is concerned with the future, is essentially designed by the decision-maker to satisfy the needs and ambitions of his *present*, to give him *now* a 'good state of mind'. For the decision-maker the future exists only in the present, in the present activity of his imagination, feed it how he will with statistics, observations and the most recent suggestions of science. A *good expectational state of mind* springs from the consciousness of having opened the doors to good fortune so far as seems consistent with keeping out the finally fatal kinds of disaster, This is the meaning of the conception of focus-values which we have put forward above, and to which we return in the next chapter to show how this construction can give an extended power to the arithmetic of discounting in explaining the low elasticity of investment with respect to the interest rate.

By the *cash flow* from a plant we mean some assumed series of its annual, weekly or momently trading revenues, where trading revenue is the excess of sale proceeds of the product of some interval over the value of inputs to the plant for its operation in the interval. Here in speaking of sale proceeds of product and value of inputs, we are supposing these sums of money to be actually received or paid in the interval. (Alternatively, sums paid or received at other times on account of the operations of this interval can be adjusted to find what they would have to be if made in the interval.) We have shown why, and how, such a dated packet of trading revenue needs to be discounted for deferment, in order that the businessman may find out how much spot cash now in hand that deferred packet means to him or represents for him. *Discounted cash flow* is another name for the businessman's valuation of his series of assumed trading revenues from a proposed plant, or in yet other words, his demand-price for that plant. In all the statements we have made in this paragraph, we have used the word 'assumed' in order to side-step the problem of uncertainty. We have shown in this chapter how that problem can be treated by discounting for uncertainty or by selection of the pay-off period, and in the next chapter we shall discuss still another method. Meanwhile we must here answer a question which the reader will legitimately wish to raise.

One word, which he may have expected to see, has made no appearance in our discussion. What part does the idea of depreciation-allowance play in investment decisions? Our answer may be found disconcerting. In the evaluation of a single plant or investment project, depreciation does not enter explicitly at all. A plant depreciates, that is, becomes less valuable, in the course of its use, as it suffers wear and tear and the cheapening of competing products from more modern and efficient plants. Such wear and tear, and such cheapening of its class of product, will in some degree have been foreseen. What has happened, when the plant is found to have a lower market value after the lapse of some part of its useful life, is that some of the instalments of trading revenue which were expected from it when it was ordered, and these perhaps the largest, have been received and are no longer part of its potential. Value is drained from it as its future passes via actuality into the past. The value thus lost, however, is not disappearing down a sink. It is part, or the whole, of the cash flow from the plant. Depreciation, in technical or market fact, is the gradual recovery from the plant of the value which was put into it at its construction. In the book-keeping sense, depreciation is the recognition that whereas when the plant was brand new it held the promise of long-continuing output at prices which at first would be relatively high, and the firm thus possessed in it a large asset, it now possesses a plant whose future useful life has become shorter and its output less highly priced, and which thus represents a smaller asset, this decline being compensated by an accumulated pile of cash, or of other things which have been bought with this cash. It may be, of course, that when all is said, and the account for this plant has been closed and its life-history can be looked back on as a record of fact, it will be seen to have fallen short of returning to the investor the whole of what it cost him to acquire it. In that case, some of the value he supposed it to have when he ordered its construction was illusory. His investment was not well judged, But if, instead, all has turned out well, the plant's depreciation is merely the living-out of its intended course of life.

However, the reader may still have objections. Is not depreciation a *cost*? To count depreciation of a contemplated plant as one of the costs of operating it, and as something to be deducted from sale-proceeds of product in arriving at trading revenues, before discounting and summing them to find a present value, would be to reckon its construction cost twice over. We must not count as a cost, both the money which the plant absorbs at its acquisition, and the money which it yields up during its useful life. The depreciation or amortization fund which will notionally be built up during that life is meant to provide for the replacement of the plant when it shall be worn out or obsolete. The instalments set aside year by year, out of trading

103

revenues, to such a fund can themselves be applied in various ways so that each grows by its own earnings, and the pace of this growth can be the fastest which the businessman feels he can count on as reliable and 'safe'. That pace need by no means be simply that of the growth of a debt at fixed interest. He may, for instance, think he can employ the instalments of the amortization fund in his own business more gainfully than by lending them on the bond market. *In any case*, it will be of concern and advantage to him to have his trading revenues come in as early as possible, for whenever they do come in he can begin to make some gainful use of them, and this he cannot do so long as they have not come in. The concentration of trading revenues in early years, and the choice of a product and a type of plant which has this effect, will be desirable, other things equal; not, however, because of any special significance of 'depreciation', but because in the most general and pervasive sense it is better to have a thing available as soon as possible: money sooner is better and bigger than the same money later.

This chapter has dwelt at much length on the businessman's problem of so formulating his investment choices that they take explicit account of the deep uncertainty on which his judgements inevitably float. We have said little of his actual thought-process of interpreting such data as he possesses into an estimate of the course of trading revenue for each possible investment. The task of describing those thoughts would be like the attempt to explain how a painter arrives at the composition of his picture. He may begin with the landscape before him, whose counterpart for the businessman is the detailed present state of his own firm and industry, a setting with its own technological and commercial texture peculiar to itself. The selection and arrangement of the elements which this landscape suggests will arise from his individual habits of mind, and those in turn from his individual psychic constitution and his individual experience of life. Both the 'business landscape' and the use he makes of it are too much a matter of particular and specialized detail to be analysed on the economist's general principles. All that these principles have to say concerns the logical relation of associated quantities when these quantities are assumed to be known, and this is the subject of Chapter 3. There we saw how a sufficient knowledge of the production-function, the factor-markets and the product-market would determine what output of a given product would make as large as possible the *net revenue* (what we are calling, in the context of investment, the *trading revenue*) from that product. Nevertheless there is an aspect of the estimation of trading revenue which we must here discuss.

If the plant or equipment-system in question is composed of a number of items similar amongst themselves (as a fleet of trucks or a number of looms or printing-presses), the investment-decision will be not only whether to invest but on what scale. There will be a best scale, namely, that which makes as large as possible the investment-gain or excess of the present value of the investment over its supply price. As the businessman passes in review a larger and larger possible scale, or more and more unit items to be simultaneously ordered, he may judge that the prospective sale proceeds from the output from each item decline while the supply-price of the inputs needed to operate the plant is perhaps pushed up, so that the trading revenues of *each* item on the whole decline. Over some range, however, this effect will be outweighed by the increase in the proposed number of items. The maximum of investment-gain for the project as a whole will be where the extra investment-gain, ascribable to the marginal unit, is zero. The inclusion of that unit will have brought into the reckoning some excess of its own discounted trading revenues over its own supply-price, and also some loss of investment-gain by the units to which this marginal unit is added. Where these two effects cancel each other, the marginal investment-gain for the plant as a whole will be zero and the total investment-gain will be a maximum.

CHAPTER 5

Expectation

Decision is choice amongst rival available courses of action. We can choose only what is still unactualized; we can choose only amongst imaginations and figments. Imagined actions and policies can have only imagined consequences, and it follows that we can choose only an action whose consequences we cannot directly know, since we cannot be eye-witnesses of them. If we knew what would be the sequel of each of the different and mutually exclusive courses open to us, we should choose the act whose sequel we most desired. Desiredness of the consequences ascribed to a course of action, when those consequences, in all respects which concern us, are taken as a whole, is one ground of preference for one course over another. If we had unquestioned and full relevant knowledge, it would be the only ground. But where there is no such knowledge, and where the nature of time itself renders the idea of such knowledge empty, there must be other considerations.

Knowledge would not deserve that name if it gave us several conflicting accounts and answered our question 'What will follow if I do this?' in more than one way. Knowledge must consist in a statement which is unique. In the absence of knowledge there is room for many answers, all of which we must provide for ourselves; and since the number of suggestions which our visible circumstances will supply, which bear on the matter, can be endless, it will be natural to construct many such answers in rivalry to each other. How are we to choose amongst rival, that is, mutually exclusive, courses of action, when each such course is assigned, not one uniquely described sequel but a skein of imagined sequels which are rivals amongst themselves?

We shall call any such suggested sequel an expectation. The qualities of an expectation, as they concern the decision-making businessman, resolve themselves into two summary characteristics. There is first the desiredness of the sequel, regardless of any question of its claim to be taken seriously. And there is that claim itself, whatever formal expression, real nature, or evidential basis we suppose it to have. The main task of the analyst of expectation is to evolve some scheme in which these three elements, the formal, the psychic and the inferential, are satisfactorily fused. This scheme must

106

in effect be able to rank or order the skeins of expectations, each taken as a whole, one skein for each course of action, so as to show why the businessman or other decision-maker chooses one course out of many possible ones.

Schemes which have been proposed for this purpose differ radically in many respects. One question is how to express and represent the force of the claim of a particular expectation to be taken seriously, what we shall call the standing of an expectation. The methods of such expression fall first into two classes. On one hand we have an analogue of statistical probability. If some operation, defined by setting bounds to the variability of certain circumstances in which it shall take place, is performed repeatedly, and if the distinct results which this operation can have are exhaustively divided under a fixed list of headings, we may be able to discover approximately in what proportion of the total number of performances the result has fallen under this or that heading. Each heading may be called a contingency, and the ratio of its occurrences to any total of performances is its probability. If each heading can be assigned a value, this value can be multiplied by the probability and the products of these multiplications for all the different headings can be added together. The total is called the mathematical expectation of the value of a series of many repetitions of the operation.

The meaning and character of this scheme need to be carefully considered. Each probability is evidently a proper fraction, and for any one defined operation with its exhaustive list of contingencies, these proper fractions must evidently sum to unity. For when we consider *all* the headings we have necessarily brought into the reckoning *all* of the results of any identified series of performances. All divided by all is one. Let us express this aspect by saying that probability is a distributional variable. It distributes the whole of the occurrences over the headings.

There are two ways in which such probabilities may be arrived at. One is by the actual performance of a long series of repetitions of the operation. The other, only available in special cases, is by discerning in the system to which the operation applies, a character of symmetry such that no one of the headings appears to have any greater power to gather in results than any other. Such a system is constituted by a pair of dice. Each die is as nearly as possible a cube made of material of uniform density. Each of its six faces bears a different number from one up to six. There is nothing in the configuration of the die or in the method of throwing it which visibly portends that it will fall with one identified face uppermost rather than another. On this ground we say that the faces of any one die are equi-probable. At this point let us note the paradoxical nature of probability; paradoxical, that is, until we make one vital distinction. For it is plain that the notion of probability depends on that of ignorance. If, when throwing a die at 8.45 a.m. on September 12, 1968, I could know what face would appear uppermost, and again when throwing the die on the next particular occasion, viz. at 8.46 a.m., I could know what face would appear, and so on, there would be no need and no room for the notion of probability. It is *ignorance* of the result which will be got from any one, identified, dated and timed throw by a particular person, which gives point to the notion of probability. Yet what are we doing when we distribute the results of one throw after another under their contingencies? We are obtaining *knowledge*. Probability is knowledge whose meaning depends on ignorance.

But the resolution of the paradox is simple. The ignorance is ignorance of the result which will be obtained from some one identified throw. The knowledge is knowledge of the collective result of a series of many throws all considered as one whole. Let us call the making of a whole series of throws a divisible experiment, and the making of a single throw an example of a non-divisible experiment. Then we assert that probability is knowledge about the outcome of a divisible experiment. About the outcome of a non-divisible experiment, probability is not knowledge but something comparable with a racing tipster's selection of a horse to win a particular race. Our system of knowledge is not destroyed when the horse fails to win. But if a divisible experiment produced a result widely different from the carefully obtained probability distribution, we should have ground for feeling disturbed. Something would have gone wrong in a way for which we should feel responsible. It may be silly to bet on a long-odds outsider for a horse race, ignoring the selection of the expert. It may be sillier still to bet heavily on his selection, if we cannot afford to lose our stake.

In the situations which arise in business life it is scarcely conceivable that a symmetry could be discerned comparable to that of the configuration of a die. Thus if probabilities are to be discovered it would have to be by repeated trials in a long series of similar situations. Business life does furnish some such possibilities. Insurance rests on this principle, so does quality control in long runs of production of standardized objects. Insurance, indeed, illuminates brilliantly what those circumstances are which render probability powerful or powerless. For the man who insures against personal disaster, the knowledge that only so-and-so many people out of every million in his situation suffer such disaster is insufficient comfort. The important word is disaster, and for him what matters is that such disaster *can* make him its victim. Long odds against it do not satisfy. For the insurance company, by contrast, probability provides knowledge. The number of accidents per year per thousand of insured may in many contexts be a fairly stable proportion, changing slowly and steadily as a consequence of social and technological evolution. Thus what is for the individual a non-divisible experiment can become in the hands of the insurance company part of a divisible one. It can be pooled with scores of thousands of others and thus the individual can exchange the certainty of a small loss (the premium on his policy) for the haunting possibility of a total one.

But when the proposed experiment consists in embodying novelty of technique or product in a plant which must be built and operated as a whole on a scale costing an appreciable part of the firm's entire resources, where can a record be found of even a few approximately relevant cases, in order to calculate a probability of success? Above all, how can such a probability have *meaning* for a firm which can only build such a plant once in twenty years? Such an investment has something of the character of a *crucial* experiment, one whose repetition is logically impossible because its very performance destroys for ever the conditions in which it was undertaken, which form an essential part of it. Novelty does not remain novel. Once illustrated in practice, an invention can be imitated. The ignorance or distrust of a new technique, once banished from the minds of a firm's rivals, can never be restored. The success of the investment may set the firm on the road to a vast expansion, or its failure may ruin the firm. These results are not reversible. The firm has a personal identity, large-scale events which happen to it are, from its viewpoint, each essentially unique. The firm needs a scheme of thought quite different from that of *averaging* the things that have happened to others; it needs a scheme which places in a strong light the worst that 'can' happen to itself, through the adoption of this investment-programme or that.

Probability seems inappropriate as the measure of the standing of a hypothesis concerning a non-divisible, and especially a crucial, experiment. A crucial experiment, where the affairs of the business-man investor in plant have come to a parting of the ways, so that one outcome would lead these affairs down one road and another outcome a quite different road, and there could never afterwards be any traverse from one road to the other, is a situation which, of its essential nature, excludes repetition. And without repetition, actual or conceivable, what applicable meaning can probability have? Let us concede that in any such operation as throwing dice, spinning the roulette-wheel or constructing a life-table, the conditions of each identified instance are not strictly identical with those of any other instance. If they were, we must suppose that the result also would be strictly the same in every instance. There is some latitude in the cir-cumstances, and it is this latitude which engenders ultimate ignorance about the outcome of any one instance. Probability expresses, indeed, a most surprising fact of Nature. The multitude of 'small' variations in many different dimensions of the phase-space, jostling each other in the collective mass of instances, produce regularity and the approximate constancy and reliability of the frequency-ratios. Much of natural science is nowadays founded upon this fascinating and, may we say, unexplained truth. The Uniformity of Nature is the statistical uniformity of great numbers of instances. Furthermore, if variability of the circumstances of a mechanical operation such as dice-throwing is an essential feature of the experiment, why should not a somewhat greater variation be allowed in a series of business operations, so that effective repetition could be secured by pooling a number of different investments which, nonetheless, could claim to have some features in common? Is it not again a matter of degree? For the largest firms (with perhaps £1000 million of assets and of annual turnover) engaged in a variety of productive lines in many places and for many widely diverse and spatially dispersed markets, this contention may have force. It remains true that the crucial experiment, in business, politics or diplomacy, destroys its own *essential* circumstances. When the battle or the election or the negotiation is won or lost, things can never be the same again. This is one source of the inappropriateness of probability for our purpose.

However, we spoke above of an *analogue* of statistical probability. If the methods of the actual counting of cases do not apply, may it not still be legitimate to use probability as a language for the expression of judgements? Such a use would have to conform to the essential character of probability, namely, the assumption that everything which can happen, by way of result of the experiment, can be placed under one or other heading of an exhaustive list of headings, so that all contingencies which are regarded as distinct from each other are defined and listed in advance. An adjudged subjective probability then takes the *form* of a ratio of the occurrences of some one contingency to the entire number of performances which constitute the experiment. We are bound to ask: Does the use of subjective probability envisage an eventual series of actual and recordable repetitions? If not, what is its mode of expressing a judgement of the standing of a hypothesis or suggested contingency? Does it assert that *if* such repetitions were conceivable the resulting frequency ratio would be such and such? What is its meaning?

The question arises whether the uncertainty-variable, or measure of the standing of a hypothesis, need be distributional. What ground has the decision-maker at any moment to assume that his stream of invention of new hypotheses has ceased? And if the potential for such invention is essentially endless, if there is in the nature of things no limit to the new insights and new uses of insights a man may evolve, how can it be legitimate to take the list of hypotheses which he has at any moment compiled in answer to some question, and arbitrarily declare it to be exhaustive and complete? If it is not exhaustive, why should he assume, and how can it be other than misleading to assume, that a distribution of *unity*, representing completeness, over the items of the list as far as it has gone can express defensible judgements? This ground of dissatisfaction with a distributional variable can be stated in other terms. We can say that when the list of hypotheses which has so far been compiled is not known, and can never be known, to be complete, it is necessary to add to it a residual hypothesis, an empty box of unknown contents, to which will be assigned the probability representing at one and the same time the possible invention of further hypotheses and the standing which these unguessable hypotheses will claim when they have been conceived. A final esoteric formulation, which may appeal to mathematicians, can be suggested. If each conceivable distinct course of events, which might be the sequel of a given present choice of action, is thought of as a function of a real variable, namely, future calendar time, we may appeal to the proposition that the cardinality of the functions of a real variable is greater than the cardinality of the real number continuum. How, then, can probabilities expressed in real numbers be assigned to the conceivable courses of events?

It is time to get in touch again with the businessman's practical frame of thought. He is surely concerned, not with an average or amalgam of many mutually exclusive or contradictory ideas of the sequel to any action of his own, only one of which ideas, at most, can in the event be approximately justified, but with estimating the worst danger to which his proposed course of action seems to expose him. There is no telling what *will* happen, it may be legitimate to form judgements of what *can* happen, at worst and at best. Let us point out at once that any such answers which the businessman may give himself are *judgements* and are *subjective*. (It is not the subjectiveness of subjective probability that we find unsatisfactory, but its distributional character.) In the last analysis, sheer, essential and incurable non-existence of knowledge, the non-existent knowledge of particulars which have not yet themselves come into existence, is a void which can be filled only by imagination, by the creation of figments. Estimation, judgement, inference, the exploitation of suggestions which the visible present and the records of the past supply, are worthy forms of language, but they must not be allowed to disguise the essential non-observability of the future. We may, then, be justified in considering what should be the characteristics of a non-distributional uncertainty-variable.

Our formal starting point for constructing a non-distributional uncertainty-variable, or measure of the standing of a hypothesis, is the requirement that the measure assigned to any particular hypothesis shall be independent of those assigned to any and all rival hypotheses. If our variable possesses this character, we shall be freed from any concern with finding a large population, actual or notional, of instances of putting the question to which the hypotheses are suggested answers. Thus we shall be able to deal with what we have called a crucial experiment, where the question is what will happen when, once for all in the most inclusive sense, some combination of circumstances is brought about which, by its nature, can never be brought about again. An experiment, let us remind ourselves, can be crucial for an identified, particular person or firm even when it is not crucial for a large collection of people or firms. But in this book we are concerned with decisions made by the individual person or firm in his own interest. By the independence of our measure we shall be also freed from concern about the possibility that further distinct hypotheses, in answer to the question, can continue to be invented endlessly, and the certainty that, save in special cases, the list can never at any named historical moment, be known and demonstrated to be complete. We shall, that is to say, be freed from any concern with the standing of a *residual hypothesis*. And thirdly, the consciousness that the endless pursuit of variants of the imaginable sequel to this or that immediate action may still leave some unthought-of variants insidiously lying in wait, need not render meaningless the measure of standing assigned to variants already thought of. We shall be able, that is, to assign various degrees of counter-expectedness to the hypotheses that we have thought of, even while we are aware that in the event we may be confronted with something which, in its specific character, was never dreamed of. Lastly, a non-distributional variable may enable us to select some hypotheses which are particularly interesting or critical for the decision-maker facing, with his given temperament and habits of thought, a particular prevailing situation. These three or four considerations constitute the case for wanting a non-distributional uncertainty-variable. What can be its nature?

Reason and instinct may enable the visible to set bounds to the invisible. There may at any epoch be a limiting practicable speed at which, if not invention, at least innovation, the embodiment of inventions in plant, can proceed. Change may accelerate, but even this acceleration may seem to have its limits. It may be reasonable for the businessman to ask himself what are the natural extremes of the range of situations which can develop within this or that length of time from the present. His appropriate question may be: What *can* happen? If so, the appropriate uncertainty-variable is some means of stating judgements of degree of *possibility*.

In their simplest form, such judgements would divide the imagined sequels of some action merely into the possible and the impossible. All those which were not entirely rejected would thus be regarded as equally possible, and no one of them would command more attention than another on the ground of conforming more to the accepted nature and habit of the world. If one such hypothesis was more attended to than another, this would be on account of its being more desired, or more counter-desired. If, then, the hypotheses were arranged in order of desiredness, we might claim that the extreme member of the series, at one end or the other, would gain the most attention. If all the sequels were looked upon as in some sense 'good', then the best of them would be the one to gain this special attention. Or if all were bad, it would be the worst. But by what test, and by comparison with what, would the sequels be judged good or bad? It seems natural that a man should compare them with his present or recent experience. A sequel is good if it is an improvement on the existing situation, bad if it is a worsening. It seems natural also to suppose that improvements or worsenings would both seem possible. But we can turn the argument round, and ask whether the significance of our existing situation does not largely reside in the situations that it can lead to? If so, the series of possible sequels, arranged in order of desiredness, would fall naturally into the good and the bad, or the desired and the counter-desired, on either side of a neutral member of the series. And our argument then leads to the conclusion that the *two* extremes of the series would claim special attention and leave the others unconsidered.

Indeed, if many different outcomes, all of them positively desired, are regarded as all *equally* possible, why should a decision-maker give weight to any but the best of them? Let us remind ourselves that we are not concerned with a divisible experiment in which it would be legitimate to think of each of the conceived outcomes as destined to prove true in some ascertainable proportion of cases. Our search is for a scheme of thought capable of dealing with a crucial, a non-divisible experiment. If all of a series of outcomes are positively disliked, it will on the same reasoning be only the worst that will count. In a series embracing both good and bad, we suggest that it is the two extreme members which will predominantly claim attention. They will be what we shall call *focus-hypotheses*.

The conception of focus-hypotheses can be variously refined. If the decision-maker has in mind some past instances, where he can remember the feeling of doubt and difficulty or the sense of a stretch of imagination, which he experienced in supposing some specific hypothesis in some specific set of circumstances to prove true (no matter whether or not it did in the subsequent event prove true) he can perhaps use these instances as graduations of a scale of disbelief, enabling him to compare any hypothesis concerning the outcome of some proposed action with one or other of these bench-marks and adjudge it 'less than perfectly possible', 'doubtfully possible', 'very difficult to suppose possible', and so on. One such level may then seem to him the lowest degree of possibility that need entitle any hypothesis to weigh with him in his decision. On this level of possibility, as on that of perfect possibility, or in the undifferentiated category of 'possible' rather than 'impossible' which we have hitherto supposed him to use, he will find a most desired and a most counter-desired hypothetical outcome. When each of these is an investment-gain, positive or negative, it will naturally be a larger positive gain, or a numerically larger loss, than the respective extreme hypotheses which stand on the 'perfectly possible' level. The shift of his attention to this alternative pair of extreme hypotheses may seem justified through the compensation of lower possibility by a more important content (numerically larger named gain or loss) of the two hypotheses.

However, suppositions of gain and of loss, even when seeming equally possible, do not play quite parallel roles in the decision-maker's thought. A loss can cripple or destroy the firm, or lead to his losing his controlling position in it. It may be that a suppositious loss will seem important at a lower level of possibility than a suppositious gain. If so, the two extreme relevant hypotheses may be found at two different levels of possibility. If such a conclusion seems untidy, this is part of the inherent untidiness of any system into which a decision-maker may compose his expectations, since such a system necessarily combines thoughts that are at odds with each other. Within the scheme of analysis that we have outlined, the decision-maker can be conceived to select first the lowest level of possibility on which he ought to pay attention to suppositions of loss; next, to ask himself what is the largest tolerable loss, in the existing circumstances of the firm; and then to search for that investment-project which offers the largest hypothetical gain for a focus-loss, at the pre-selected level of possibility, not larger than this limit.

The mode of statement of his expectations that we are ascribing to the decision-maker can be given a more unified and coherent form by treating each of its three elements as a continuous variable. Let us suppose any hypothesis about the sequel of some present action to be represented for him merely by the monetary gain or loss, x, which it implies. Let the degree of possibility he assigns to any such hypothesis be represented by the degree of surprise, y, which on present evidence he now thinks he would feel if this hypothesis were justified in the event. Such potential surprise evidently measures possibility in an inverse manner. Total rejection of a hypothesis as impossible will be expressed by an absolute maximum degree $\bar{y}$ of potential surprise, while the ascription of perfect possibility will be expressed by zero potential surprise $y = 0$. We suppose that between these two extremes, remembered experiences will provide bench-marks by which the graduations of a scale of surprise can be located. Lastly, the decision-maker's degree of concern with any specified outcome, x, having regard to the degree, y, of potential surprise or inverse possibility which he ascribes to it, will be called its ascendancy. The ascendancy, A, of any hypothesis may be thought of as its power to arrest the decision-maker's attention as he passes in review a range of diverse outcomes. We shall assume that this power is greater, the greater the size of gain, or of loss, named by the hypothesis, and that it is smaller, the higher the degree of potential surprise assigned to the hypothesis. Each outcome, x, may evidently represent or be able to arise from any one of a number of distinct courses of events. In such a case it is the most possible of these courses of events which will determine the degree of possibility ascribed to the outcome in question. Let us notice that in our construction, the plurality of routes (that is, distinct imagined courses of events) through whose actualization a given gain or loss, x, could come to pass, does not concern us unless in some way it is supposed to increase the possibility of that outcome. But if, for example, any one route leading to that outcome is itself regarded by the decision-maker as perfectly possible, no number of additional routes can improve that degree of possibility.

Our three variables are now as follows:

x a size of gain or loss named as a hypothesis.

y the potential surprise assigned to the hypothesis x.

A the ascendancy, or power of a hypothesis, x, to engender the decision-maker's interest or concern.

We wish to derive the general character of a function connecting with each other these three variables. This function must express both the dependence of A on x directly, its dependence on y, and the dependence of y on x. Let us begin with this latter aspect.

If the decision-maker envisages a wide diversity of sets of circumstances from any one of which the sequel to his present action may arise (sets of circumstances in any one of which, for example, his proposed plant may have to produce and sell its output), values of x ranging from large gains to large losses may all seem perfectly and equally possible. For all of these, y will be zero. Beyond the extremes of this inner range, numerically increasing values of x (larger and larger supposititious gains or larger and larger supposititious losses) will

115

carry increasingly sceptical judgements of possibility, that is, increasing associated values of y. At some size of gain, and at some size of loss, this scepticism will amount to entire rejection, and at these sizes of x, and beyond them, the assigned values of y will be an absolute maximum. If these considerations are valid, the typical form of a curve connecting y with x will be that of a vertical section through the middle of a flat-bottomed basin, as in Fig. 5.1.

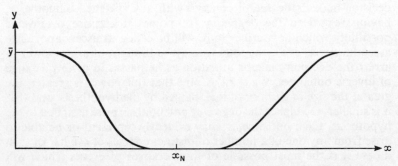

The potential surprise curve of some investment. x_N the neutral outcome, taken to be $x = 0$.

FIG. 5.1

We have defined the neutral outcome as that hypothesis concerning the sequel of present action, whose realization would be deemed by the decision-maker neither an improvement nor a deterioration of his situation. We have argued also that the neutral outcome will not lie near either extreme of the range of outcomes which are judged to be possible, but in the midst of them. In terms of our variable, x, the neutral outcome will evidently be $x = 0$, and according to our argument, will somewhere divide the 'perfectly possible' values of x into a positive and a negative range. Thus the 'bottom of the basin', that segment of the y-curve for which $y(x) = 0$, will lie along the x-axis and will have the neutral outcome $x = 0$ somewhere in its interior. Outside this inner range, at either end, there will be a further range where the curve bends away from the x-axis north-eastwards or north-westwards, and on these horns of the curve, represented by the sloping sides of the basin, we shall have $dy/dx > 0$ (the slope will be positive) for $x > 0$ and $dy/dx < 0$ (the slope will be negative) for $x < 0$. Ultimately some positive and some negative value of x will be reached where possibility vanishes and the y-curve reaches the line $y = \bar{y}$. There is no reason in general why the two branches of the curve on either side of $x = 0$ should be even approximately sym-

116

metrical. We can suggest only that they will be broadly similar, when the algebraic sign of x is neglected.

Let us turn now to the dependence of A on x and on y. A large loss will be of more serious concern to the decision-maker than a small one, and a large gain will be of more interest than a small one. The ascendancy of any hypothetical outcome, that is to say, will be an increasing function of the numerical size of that outcome, and we can write

$$\partial A/\partial x > 0 \quad \text{for} \quad x > 0$$

$$\partial A/\partial x < 0 \quad \text{for} \quad x < 0$$

Instead of the second of these expressions we could define, say, $z = -x$ and write $\partial A/\partial z > 0$. An outcome which the decision-maker dismisses as impossible will be of no concern to him, so that

$$A(x, \bar{y}) = 0$$

It seems natural to suppose that his concern with any imagined outcome will be less, the less the possibility, or the higher the potential surprise, that he assigns it, and we can write

$$\partial A/\partial y < 0 \quad \text{for all } x.$$

The effect of all these assumptions when they are brought together will best be seen geometrically. To represent our three variables on two dimensions, we must again resort to contour lines. These equal-ascendancy curves will be drawn in a diagram (Fig. 5.2) whose east–west axis shows values of x and whose north–south axis shows values of y. The relevant range of the y-axis will be bounded by the values $y = 0$ and $y = \bar{y}$, and thus the equal ascend-

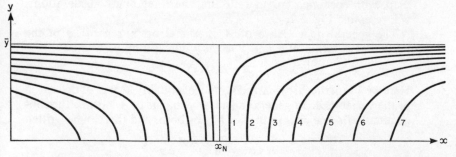

An equal-ascendancy map. Curves numbered in increasing sequence represent increasing degrees of ascendancy.

FIG. 5.2

117

ancy curves must lie completely within this zone. Each equal-ascendancy curve will connect points (x, y) such that the corresponding values of A are all equal, but as we move eastwards or westwards along the x-axis away from the neutral outcome we shall encounter contours representing successively higher degrees of ascendancy. The equal-ascendancy curves, where their ends rest on the x-axis, will thus form two ladders of increasing degrees of ascendancy rising from the neutral outcome where, amongst outcomes associated with perfect possibility, the interest and concern of the decision-maker will be at its least. Each such ladder, one rising to the eastward, the other to the westward of the neutral outcome, reflects our assumption that A is everywhere an increasing function of the numerical sizes of x.

We have so interpreted ascendancy as to make it zero for all outcomes looked on as impossible. If we think it natural also to make ascendancy zero for an outcome which merely, in the decision-maker's view, preserves the current situation, we shall have $A = 0$ at the neutral outcome even for perfect possibility, and one of the equal-ascendancy curves will be a straight north–south segment running from $y = 0$ to $y = \bar{y}$. The general typical shape of all other equal-ascendancy curves is suggested by taking in conjunction with each other three considerations. First, such a curve represents a greater-than-zero level of A; secondly, it must slope north-eastwards or north-westwards in order that increasing values of y may compensate increasing numerical values of x so as to keep A constant along any one curve; and thirdly, A is zero everywhere on the line $y = \bar{y}$, so that no equal ascendancy curve for $A > 0$ can ever attain that line. Such curves accordingly must be broadly concave to the x-axis, bending more and more eastwards or westwards, and having a less and less northward direction, as x increases numerically, so that they approach the line $y = \bar{y}$ asymptotically. An equal-ascendancy map, with specimen curves reflecting the foregoing considerations, will resemble Fig. 5.2.

The general dependence of A on x and on y, regardless of the mutual association of x and y in the y-curve, may be written

$$A \equiv A\ (x, y).$$

Here we adopt the three-barred symbol of equality by way of definition of the variable A. In general again, any change of A must be the concomitant of some change in x or in y or both, and this can be written

$$\Delta A \equiv \frac{\partial A}{\partial x}\Delta x + \frac{\partial A}{\partial y}\Delta y$$

This expression reads: the total differential of A is the sum of two terms, each of which is the product of the partial derivative of x or of

y with the change of x or of y, respectively. Now since A is unchanging along the whole of an equal-ascendancy curve, the total differential of A, when we consider only those points which lie on one such curve, is everywhere zero, and we have in consequence

$$\frac{\partial A}{\partial x}\Delta x + \frac{\partial A}{\partial y}\Delta y = 0$$

or, dividing through by Δx,

$$\frac{\partial A}{\partial x} + \frac{\partial A}{\partial y}\frac{\Delta y}{\Delta x} = 0$$

and in the limit as Δx tends to zero,

$$\frac{\partial A}{\partial x} + \frac{\partial A}{\partial y}\frac{dy}{dx} = 0$$

so that

$$\frac{dy}{dx} = -\frac{\partial A}{\partial x}\Big/\frac{\partial A}{\partial y} \tag{5.1}$$

Since we conceive every point of the surface $A \equiv A(x,y)$ to be contained in some one or other equal-ascendancy curve, the relation (5.1) will be true everywhere on this surface.

We have considered the character of the dependence of A on x and on y, and that of the dependence of y on x. Now we can put these two sets of considerations together. An equal ascendancy curve, though involving the dependence of A on x and on y, effectively implies an association of values of x and of y with each other. In principle we could solve the equation

$$A(x, y) \equiv \text{constant}$$

and make the implicit mutual dependence of x and y explicit, writing, say,

$$y \equiv f(x, A)$$

Thus it is plain that the equal-ascendancy curves, though their meaning is that of contours of a surface, can be conceived as drawn in the xy-plane just as is the y-curve. We can in fact superpose the y-curve on the equal-ascendancy map as in Fig. 5.3 and by this means illustrate the character of those focus outcomes which we are in search of.

Each potential surprise curve must be deemed unique. Each is the statement of the judgements of a particular individual concerning the degrees of possibility of an array of rival hypothetical outcomes of an investment-proposal. Thus each such curve belongs to one specific investment scheme and no other, and is in a sense a description of an aspect of that scheme. Likewise each equal-ascendancy map must be deemed unique. Each such map is a description of an aspect of an individual mind. It states that mind's valuation of sizes of gain and loss and of the degrees of possibility ascribed to them, a valuation in terms of their significance for his firm and its policies. The question which particular combinations of size of hypothetical gain and loss, and degrees of possibility, are *relevant* cannot be answered until the surprise-curve of a particular investment-proposal has been applied to the ascendancy surface of the individual who has conceived that proposal and has laid out its surprise-curve. This is the significance of the superposing of the two diagrams one on another. However, before we consider how this superposition delivers its message, we may look at a much more direct and intimate fusion of the two functions, the y-curve and the A-surface. For the A-surface is written $A \equiv A(x,y)$, and y in turn ought for our purpose to be written $y = y(x)$. So we have $A \equiv A\{x,y(x)\}$ which reads: A is a function of x and of y which is itself a function of x.

The formula $A \equiv A\{x,y(x)\}$ is the equation of what is known in England as a twisted curve, and in the United States as a space-curve. To see the meaning of these expressions, let us imagine the surface $A \equiv A\ (x,y)$ in its full three-dimensional being, rather than merely as a family of contours projected on to the xy-plane. We may imagine these contours, or specimens of them, as being traced on the surface itself, as though a white mark was traced on an actual mountain-side to join points of equal altitude. Let us further imagine a wall, perpendicular to the xy-plane, to be erected along the length of the y-curve which we suppose, as before, to be traced on the xy-plane. This wall will intersect the A-surface in a path which will bend in two dimensions. It will bend in the y-dimension according to the bending of the y-curve away from the x-axis, and it will bend in the A-dimension according to the slope of the A-surface where it rises higher above the xy-plane or falls nearer to it. This path is the twisted curve $A \equiv A\{x,y(x)\}$, and if the A-surface were a real mountain-side we could imagine ourselves to follow this path from $x = 0, y = 0$ through, say, increasing positive values of x. Along that segment where y is zero, A will increase monotonically with x and the path will steadily rise, though not necessarily at a constant slope. Where the y-curve bends away from the x-axis, a fresh influence comes into play. Here A is still pressed upwards by increasing sizes of supposed gain, but its rise is restrained with increasing strength by the concomitant decrease of adjudged possibility, and eventually, because A must decline to zero where y becomes equal to $\bar{y}$, that rise must be halted and reversed. Let us suppose that reversal takes place in a single point (x, y), a single 'summit' of the path. Such a summit is a maximum, and at that point the derivative of the function $A \equiv A\ \{x,y(x)\}$ will be zero. We have

$$\frac{dA\{x, y(x)\}}{dx} \equiv \frac{\partial A}{\partial x} + \frac{\partial A}{\partial y}\frac{dy}{dx}$$

When this is put equal to zero we have

$$\frac{dy}{dx} = -\frac{\partial A}{\partial x}\bigg/\frac{\partial A}{\partial y}$$

But this is the self-same expression that we obtained from an equal ascendancy curve by considering the fact that its total differential is everywhere zero. It follows that at the summit of the twisted curve, its north-eastward trend will be the same as that of the equal-ascendancy curve which passses through that point of the A-surface. At that point, the two curves will have a point in common, and they will be parallel. Thus they will at that point be tangent to each other.

The two tangencies of a potential surprise-curve with equal-ascendancy curves, one on each side of the neutral outcome, appear

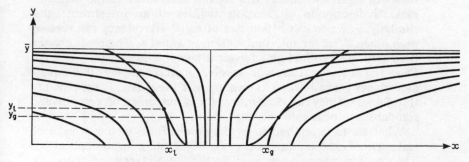

y_l degree of potential surprise of focus loss.
y_g degree of potential surprise of focus gain.
x_l standardized focus loss.
x_g standardized focus gain.

FIG. 5.3

in Fig. 5.3. Let us remind ourselves that the presence of an equal-ascendancy curve in just the right place to be tangent to the y-curve is no accident. Every point of the surface $A \equiv A(x, y)$ lies on such a curve, and thus that point which happens to be the highest attained by the twisted curve amongst positive values of x, and its other summit (not in general having the same value of A) amongst negative values of x, necessarily find themselves on such curves. We have merely selected, and actually drawn, those particular equal-ascendancy curves which pass through the points in question.

121

At the stage we have now reached the reader may well ask whether these refinements result in much improvement of our scheme over its cruder version, in which we simply spoke of the decision-maker's choosing a particular level, or levels, of possibility as the ones which seemed to satisfy his temperamental and judgemental needs, and took the extreme hypotheses lying on these levels. The refined version does, however, dissolve two objections which can be brought against the cruder one. First it can be asked whether the decision-maker ought to treat as comparable two hypotheses, or two outcomes, to which he assigns different degrees of possibility. Is it legitimate, or better, is it psychically satisfying, to take as the 'promise' of a given investment, an outcome having a different assigned possibility from that of its 'threat'? Secondly, there is the question which of two outcomes on, say, the 'gain' side, having equal ascendancy through different combinations of size and possibility, is the relevant one? Both these questions disappear when we notice that, by the meaning of 'ascendancy', any two gain-hypotheses of equal ascendancy can replace each other in the decision-maker's description of the potentialities of an investment; and similarly, any two loss-hypotheses of equal ascendancy can replace each other. Thus for any combination of x and y, where y is greater than zero, we can find an equivalent combination where y is zero. Diagrammatically, this will involve merely tracing the equal-ascendancy curve down to its meeting with the x-axis. The two points thus found we may call *standardized* focus-outcomes, or, respectively, standardized focus gain and loss.

What we have referred to as the cruder form of our scheme of statement of expectations requires no further steps for its application. The decision-maker is conceived to list those investment proposals which, on some level of possibility chosen as the relevant one, give a tolerable extreme hypothesis of loss (one which would not bankrupt or paralyse the firm) and amongst these to select the one with the highest extreme hypothesis of gain, on the same level of possibility or on another level which may seem appropriate for hopes of gain. In the more refined (we do not say more practical or applicable) version, a further stage of argument may provide useful theoretical insights.

The *investment indifference map* applies, in the choice amongst investment proposals, the same technique as that which the consumer's indifference-map applies in the choice amongst combinations of quantities of consumer's goods. Instead of quantities of some commodity, distances along the east–west axis represent, in the investment-indifference map, the standardized focus losses of various investment-proposals. Distances on the north–south axis represent their standardized focus gains. Evidently an investment-indifference curve will run in a broadly south-west to north-east direction, instead of the north-west to south-east trend of a consumer's indifference curve. One investment-proposal will be preferred to another, if it lies on an investment-indifference curve which is to the north and to the west of that which contains the other. However, there is much more to be suggested about the detailed character of the investment-indifference curves than their positive slope (in contrast with the negative slope of the consumer's indifference curves). For an investment-indifference map is itself unique and peculiar to one individual, and is a reflection of that personal and individual cast of mind which has been bequeathed to him by his heredity and the earliest biochemical life of his brain, and developed by his life-history and total experience. For our purpose, and with the categories at our disposal, we must be content to distinguish the audacious from the cautious temperament.

If we suppose that the businessman will be able to bring to a stop at any moment the operation of a plant whose trading revenue has become negative, and if we suppose him to make some provision, as part of the sum he is ready to invest in it, for an initial period of trading loss while the plant is being run in, then the most he can lose by deciding to construct this plant is its construction-cost including this cost of getting it on-stream. The sum of money that, at worst, he stands to lose can on these suppositions be known to him. In the diagram of the investment-indifference map (Fig. 5.4) we therefore erect a north–south line at a point s on the east–west focus-loss axis

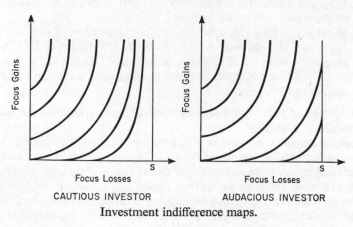

CAUTIOUS INVESTOR   AUDACIOUS INVESTOR

Investment indifference maps.

FIG. 5.4

representing, by its distance from the origin, a loss equal to the whole sum available to be invested in the plant. This investible sum may be the firm's entire resources. To the east of this barrier, investment-indifference curves will have no meaning and will therefore not exist. There are now two broad possibilities. The investment-indifference curves as they trend north-eastward may attain the total-loss barrier, or they may only approach it asymptotically. The businessman may feel that the possible loss of the whole of his investible sum can be contemplated, if only the prize of the possible gain is big enough. Or he may feel that no such prize, however big, would compensate for the possibility of total loss. Now if each investment-indifference curve must along its whole course slope north-eastward, yet must never reach the total-loss barrier, it must necessarily be broadly convex to the loss-axis and to the barrier, and bend more and more towards the north as we trace it away from the axes. If this convexity imposes itself in the case of a businessman of the type we are calling 'cautious' it seems reasonable to think that even the 'audacious' investing decision-maker will require each equal step of increase in his possible loss to be compensated by increasing steps in his possible gain, so that for him also, the indifference-curves will trend increasingly northwards. In his case, however, they will eventually meet the total loss barrier. Fig. 5.4 shows the two types of investment indifference map.

We shall discuss four particular questions which lend themselves to treatment by means of the investment-indifference map:

1. What influences govern the scale of proposed investments in plant?
2. Why can it be attractive to a firm to borrow money so as to make its resources exceed its fortune?
3. What is it which sets a bound to the extent of such borrowing?
4. How can the derivative of a flow of investment-orders, with respect to the rate of interest, be negative? That is to say, how can a fall (for example) in the rate of interest have the effect of *discouraging* investment?

For several of these questions we need the conception of the scale-opportunity curve.

Let us consider a plant of what we have called the mixing-bowl type, where sets of quantities of other factors of production can be combined in any proportions (over some ranges of such proportions) and will then produce an output depending in size purely on the quantities of these other factors, and not at all on the relation of these quantities to the capacity of the 'mixing bowl' excepting only that this capacity sets a definite physical limit to the output which can be produced. The presence of the mixing bowl is a necessary condition for the other factors to be employed and to produce output. Any difference between the expense for these other factors, and the sale proceeds of the product, will be a trading profit or loss for the plant for some time-interval of stated length and date. Any series of such trading profits, which the businessman ascribes to the proposed plant, will have a determinate 'present value' when each instalment is discounted at the going market interest rate for debts deferred to the date of the instalment. The excess, positive or negative, of such a present value over the supply-price of the plant, is what we mean by an investment gain or loss. Amongst the hypotheses of investment gain which seem to the businessman possible in this or that degree, he will be able to determine the two standardized focus outcomes, one a gain and the other a loss. If we now suppose him to plot such a pair of quantities, in the form of a point on the investment-indifference map, for each size of 'mixing bowl' over some continuous range of variation of this size, we shall have what we mean by a scale-opportunity curve. What influences seem likely to govern the shape of such a curve?

Our assumption that the plant itself plays the part of a mixing bowl only is intended to exclude *internal economies of large scale*. If every means of production, whose quantity does affect the size of the output, can be varied in quantity by as small steps as we wish, so that every quantity in any set of such quantities can be increased in one and the same ratio as all the others no matter what ratio we select for this purpose, there seems to be no reason why an increase of all factor quantities in a ration N should not increase the output in this ratio N. If so, we can say that the scale of a mixing-bowl plant has no technological effect, and the shape of the scale-opportunity curve must depend on market factors. If then, we further assume that the firm buys or hires all its means of production, other than the plant itself, in perfectly competitive factor-markets, so that the price per unit of any factor is independent of the quantity bought per time-unit by this firm, and if the construction-cost of the plant is proportional to its capacity, and if, finally, the product is to be sold in a perfectly competitive product-market, so that its price per unit is independent of the output, it seems that there is nothing to prevent the scale-opportunity curve from being a straight line. The interpretation of such a form would be that the influences and circumstances which seem to the businessman to bear on the question of the size and algebraic sign of his investment-outcome are the same per unit scale of plant, no matter whether the plant is large or small.

It may be asked whether the straight-line type of scale-opportunity curve is confined to the mixing-bowl situation, or whether a plant optimally adapted to make use of a given set of quantities of other factors might not be replaced by one which is in the relevant respects 'twice as big', when every one of the other factors has its quantity doubled; or by one which is three times as big when the other quantities are trebled; and so on. There must surely be many situations where this is the case. The hay-cart, for example, may ideally require three men to load it: one to lead the horse, two to toss up the hay. Two men perhaps can manage, but the horse and the cart will be suffering a waste of their time. If there are nine men, three horses and carts can be used; and so on. Evidently we cannot use one-and-a-third horses and carts in order to employ four men. But the adjustability of scale of plant (number of horses and carts) to the quantity available of other factors may be good enough to be well suggested by a straight continuous line. The distinction between this type of situation and that of the mixing bowl is perhaps tenuous. But this variant shows that the application of straight-line scale-opportunity curves, or of somewhat blurred and generalized mixing-bowl situations, is fairly wide. Let us remind ourselves that we are here concerned with *proposals* for investment, and hence can claim the full freedom of the long period.

It may be that as he passes in review plants of larger and larger scale but of identical technology, the businessman will recognize at some stage the possibility of substituting a different design, giving a larger output for the same quantities of other factors. This improved-technology plant, only available, we may assume, at not less than a certain scale, may cost more than the inferior-technology plant producing an equal output. For this reason it may expose the investor to a larger focus loss. But because of its economy of other factors it may also offer a larger focus gain. Its representative point on the invest-ment-indifference map may lie far off the line of the scale-opportuni-ties of the inferior plant. The improved plant may have a scale-opportunity line of its own, lying at a different angle to the axes from that of the inferior plant. It is evident that a great range of situations of varying complexity can be accommodated on the investment-indifference map, all of them reflecting a particular individual's judgements based on his personal interpretation of evidence which may be in many respects private to himself and his firm.

When we relax the assumption of perfect competition in the firm's product market, it seems very difficult to find any general considera-tions bearing on the question of the effect of this relaxation on the scale-opportunity curve. It may be that a plant restricted in scale to what is required for a local market which the firm has securely monopolized will seem to be well protected against loss, while a plant which cannot sell its capacity output unless it captures new markets may seem very hazardous. In this case the eastern range of the scale opportunity curve will be concave to the loss-axis. By contrast it may be that large scale, if it involves geographical spread of markets and supplies, will be looked upon as a safeguard, so that the scale-opportunity curve will bend northwards. Some scale-opportunity situations are illustrated in Fig. 5.5.

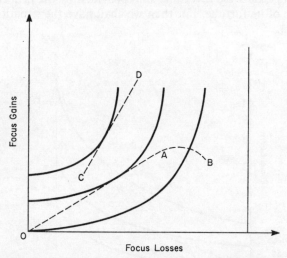

OA: segment of a scale opportunity curve corresponding to perfect competition in product and factor markets, and to absence of economies of large scale.

AB: segment corresponding to imperfectly competitive markets.

CD: a plant of higher efficiency but with a minimum practicable scale.

FIG. 5.5

The scale-opportunity curve is, of course, meant to be used in conjunction with an investment-indifference map. That scale of plant will be chosen which places the investment on the highest attainable investment-indifference curve. If the indifference curves are concave northwards, while the scale-opportunity curve is straight or concave southwards towards the loss-axis, there may be a point of tangency representing this optimal scale. If so, the indifference-opportunity diagram will be suggesting that the scale of investment in a plant of a given type is limited by the increasing danger to the firm entailed by increasing the ratio of focus loss to the firm's fortune or to the sum available for investment. This is one type of answer to our question 1 on page 124. However, there is another possibility. The investible sum which the firm sets aside out of its own fortune may not be the

127

whole of the resources which it can make available for the investment. It can borrow at fixed interest, and if such borrowing takes the form of a mortgage on the plant which is to be constructed, the firm may be able to transfer some of the risk of the investment to the lenders. This will be possible (supposing the lenders to be willing) if the loan is secured solely on the new plant, and not at all on the rest of the firm's assets; or if the investible sum provided by the firm represents the whole of its fortune. For then we shall have the situation shown in Fig. 5.6.

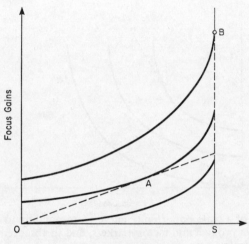

The eastward distance OS is a loss equal to the whole sum available for investment in the plant. Point A is the most desired combination of focus gain and loss attainable without borrowing. Point B may be attainable if lenders for an appropriate sum can be found.

FIG. 5.6

Here we see the scale-opportunity curve carried right across as far as the barrier which represents the loss of the whole of the sum available for investment. What happens next, after we have traced it as far as that barrier? There can be no tracing it beyond the barrier, for according to the meaning of the barrier, the scale-opportunity curve can have no meaning to the eastward of it. But we can trace the scale-opportunity curve due northwards *up* the barrier. For if extra resources can be borrowed on the security of the plant alone, these will increase the attainable scale of the plant and thus its focus gains for the firm, but will not increase its focus loss for the firm. For the firm's greatest possible loss is represented by the barrier.

128

This conception raises a number of questions. To the businessman (the firm) it must appear that those who lend to him so as to increase his total invested sum beyond the amount that he himself is willing to place at risk, and in doing so increase the focus loss of the investment, as well, beyond his own stake, stand to lose part of the sum they lend. If so, what induces them to do this? It may be, of course, that the lenders' judgement is different from the firm's, and that in their judgement the focus loss of the investment is less than the firm's own stake by an amount greater than what they are being asked to lend. But if, even in their own judgement, the lenders are exposing themselves to part of the danger inherent in investment, they will require some compensation in the form of a payment beyond the market interest rate on 'perfectly secure' loans. The greater the proportion which the lenders deem to be at risk, out of the whole amount they lend, the higher will the combined rate of interest-cum-risk premium be on the loan as a whole. On each extra 'slice' of loan (that is, *at the margin*) the rate will be higher than on the interior slices: the marginal combined rate will be an increasing function of the size of the loan. Plainly a point must come where it will not be attractive to the firm to borrow any larger sum; not a point in *time*, for as the firm's fortune grows, so its own stake in each investment, or the frequency of its operations of acquiring extra plant, can increase; but when, at some one date or in a brief period, the businessman passes in review a series of larger and larger possible sizes for his plant, attainable by means of larger and larger loans needing to be compared to his firm's given fortune at that moment, each extra £50000, needing to have its contribution to trading revenues discounted at a higher rate than the previous £50000 is likely to add less and less to the focus gain, until this difference becomes negligible. The higher discount rate to be applied at each upward step of borrowing and of scale of the plant, will affect any series of extra trading revenues which may form part of any hypothesis about the trading outcome of operating the plant. The relevant series is that one which, determined with regard to the discount rates which will apply, constitutes the focus gain. The focus loss is not relevant, since it has by supposition already exceeded the firm's largest proposed stake in the plant.

The ratio of a firm's borrowed resources to its own fortune is what is meant by writers on company finance when they speak of the gearing of a firm's capital structure. In the firm's published accounts, this capital structure will be stated as the sums of money which it obtained at various dates from various sources, as by subscription from the shareholders, from lending by debenture-holders, from the placing of part of the firm's earnings to reserve, and so on. These sums may no longer be closely related to the market worth of the firm's assets. Nonetheless the idea of gearing is present, whether we look at the ratio of borrowed to subscribed capital, or at the ratio of borrowings to the rest of the market value of the firm's assets. The effects of gearing have been discussed by M. Kalecki[1] by means of a quite different frame of concepts from those of our foregoing account, and since this other frame has a very general application to problems of investment, we shall now consider it.

The notion which Irving Fisher called the rate of return over cost, which Keynes called the marginal efficiency of capital, and which Kalecki called the marginal rate of profit, is one and the same notion. Let us for a time abandon the focus-values scheme, and again suppose the businessman to formulate his appraisal of a possible investment in the form of a 'best guess' about the trading revenue of each future year, each such amount being somewhat reduced by way of recognition of its uncertainty. We defined *investment-gain* as the excess (positive or negative) of the value of a series of trading revenues ascribed to some proposed plant (no matter whether these trading revenues represent a focus gain, a focus loss, or a 'best guess') calculated by discounting the instalments at prevailing market interest rates, over the construction cost of the plant. Now, instead, taking the 'best guess' series, let us suppose the question to be put: what percentage per annum would have to be used for discounting this series of trading revenues (one and the same percentage for all of them) in order to bring their total present value to equality with the construction cost? If this question proves to have one and only one answer, that answer is what is meant by the rate of return over cost or the marginal efficiency or marginal rate of profit. If for some particular years in the series the assumed trading revenue is negative, and if these years of negative revenue tend to alternate with years or stretches of positive revenue, there may be more than one answer to the question. However, it is difficult to know what circumstances, visible at the time of making his investment-decision, could suggest to the businessman the relevance of a hypothesis that trading revenues would fluctuate in algebraic sign. We shall therefore not spend time on this possibility.

Notationally we can express the marginal efficiency of capital as follows. Let $Q_1, Q_2, \ldots, Q_N$ be the assumed trading revenues of year 1, year 2, ..., year N, and let s be the construction cost of the plant. Then the marginal efficiency of capital is that value of m which satisfies

---

[1] 'The Principle of Increasing Risk', Chapter 4 of *Economic Fluctuations* by M. Kalecki (George Allen & Unwin, 1939).

$$s = \sum_{i=1}^{N} Q_i (1+m)^{-i}$$

In his *General Theory of Employment, Interest and Money* Keynes suggested that the total value of investment orders (orders for equipment), given per unit of time by businessmen all taken together, would always be such as to bring the marginal efficiency of capital to equality with the prevailing market interest rate. We can interpret this as the proposition that the flow of investment in plant of all kinds, in the society as a whole, will at all times be pushed to or held at that size which reduces to zero the investment-gain on the marginal (the least gainful) item in each businessman's list of simultaneously given investment orders. The mechanism by which an increase in the investment-flow is supposed to reduce the marginal efficiency of capital depends mainly on its raising the supply-prices of equipment goods through the pressure it puts on the capacity of equipment-making industries. In the equation above, it is evident that with a given series of Q's, an increase in s will reduce m. But Keynes's theory entirely neglects the influence of a change in the size of the flow of investment orders on the series of Q's assumed by each businessman in regard to his own type of equipment. We cannot here enter in detail into an explanation of the so-called 'multiplier'. But anything which raises the prices of a large range of products is plainly likely to make business in general seem more promising of gain. At least we can say that the assumption that, for any one businessman, and for the businessmen taken together, the Q's are independent of s is highly questionable.

Kalecki's *principle of increasing risk* is not exposed to the foregoing objection, since it deals with the calculations or judgements of one businessman at a time, and it is no doubt legitimate, except in the case of very large firms, to suppose that the investment orders placed by any one firm will be decided on without explicit consideration of their own effect on the prices, delivery dates, etc., of equipment of the type in question. Kalecki measures on the east–west axis of his diagram the sizes amongst which the businessman is choosing for the investment programme which he has in mind at some named historical date, or in relation to some named calendar interval whose threshold he is approaching. This size is of course a variable stated in terms of its total money cost. On the north–south axis he puts the percentage per annum which combines the market interest rate for loans to a borrower of unquestioned solvency, and the lender's required compensation for exposing himself to some risk of loss. The rate of such compensation which the lender will call for on a marginal addition to his loan will be higher, the higher the proportion which that loan already represents of the assets on which it is secured. If those assets are to consist wholly of the investment programme now in contemplation, and if the firm's own contribution to the cost of the programme is settled, the size of the programme will be governed by the marginal cost of borrowing, for at some size that cost will exceed the marginal efficiency of the extra plant which can be bought with the marginal loan. Kalecki's diagram is represented in our Fig. 5.7 from page 100 of his book *Economic Fluctuations*.

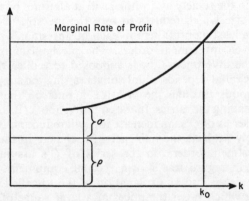

Kalecki's diagram of the principle of increasing risk.

FIG. 5.7

We come now to the last of our questions on page 124. How can a fall in the rate of interest, which, as we showed in Chapter 4, must increase the present value of any series of positive deferred trading revenues, possibly have the effect of discouraging investment? The answer depends on the possibility that some hypothesized trading revenues will be negative. For simplicity let us suppose that an entire series of trading revenues, which the businessman regards as one possible sequel to his investing in a specified design and scale of plant, is negative throughout up to a date when he would abandon operations. Such an out-turn could occur if he were prepared for some months or years of trading loss while experimenting with his plant's technical capabilities and his product's market possibilities, before finally deciding that his judgement in making the investment had been at fault and that he must stop its operation. Now the effect of a decrease in the percentage per annum at which any deferred payment is discounted is to increase the numerical size of the present value of that payment. The question whether the undiscounted sum itself, and its present value, are to be looked on as positive or negative

132

is entirely irrelevant to the numerical effects of discounting. It depends on whether they are looked at from the payer's or the receiver's viewpoint. The algebraic sign of the sums involved comes into the picture if they are of *differing* sign, for then a change in the percentage per annum used for discounting may either increase or decrease the algebraic sum of the present values, according to the character of the distribution of the undiscounted payments over future time, and to the relative sizes of these payments. If, as we are now supposing, all the deferred sums in question are losses, their present value will also represent a loss, and a reduction of the rate used for discounting them will numerically increase that loss. If the *investment focus loss* of the proposed plant corresponds to such a trading out-turn, where all trading revenues are negative, it follows that the investment focus loss will be made numerically larger by a fall in the interest rate. In terms of the investment indifference-map, this means that the point representing the investment will be moved eastwards. The investment focus gain may, of course, by the same change of the interest rate be moved northwards. Because of the southward convexity of the investment indifference curves, such a north-eastwards movement of the point representing the investment can easily carry it to a less desired indifference-curve, as shown in Fig. 5.8.

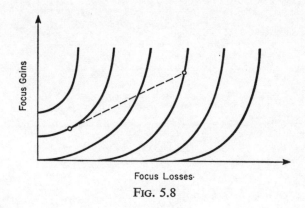

Focus Losses

FIG. 5.8

It is by no means necessary, in order that this effect may occur, for the investment focus loss to assume that all trading revenues will be negative or zero. If the negative instalments of trading revenue are concentrated at a deferment which, in number of years, is near to the reciprocal of the interest rate, while the positive instalments lie in the very near future or else far beyond the interest-reciprocal date, a change in the interest rate will affect negative instalments of a given size to a greater absolute extent than positive instalments of the same size. The effect of a fall of the interest rate can thus be, in this type of time-distribution of trading gains and losses, to discourage investment.

CHAPTER 6

Interdependent Decision-making

The monopolist or monopolistic competitor who lowers his price in the expectation of selling more is counting on a response from others to his own action. Those others, however, may include other sellers whose own prices, lowered because he has lowered his, will lessen the extent of his increase of sales. If the market for some type of commodity or for the means of satisfying some class of needs (transportation, entertainment, warmth) is shared by only a few suppliers, the actions of one may have very noticeable effects on the sales of the others, and their riposte may be correspondingly vigorous. Our firm's awareness of this possibility may modify its choice of policy or particular action. What is the essential difference between the two classes of situation, that of the firm facing many buyers and many competitors, and that of the one with few competitors, or even with few buyers? In both cases, the question what is our firm's best policy can only be answered in the light of some assumption or belief about the response of others. But when the others are a large number of buyers, each taking only a small fraction of our firm's output, their reaction to a given price change can be more easily and confidently estimated, than when the others include a few rival suppliers. And the source of this difference is the rival suppliers' recognition of their own power to influence appreciably the circumstances of our firm's selling operations.

Each single buyer out of many thousands is likely to take our firm's action as a datum. Whatever such a buyer did, the firm would remain unaware of it. When his response, consulting his own perhaps stable needs, is pooled with those of thousands of others, the result may be broadly predictable. But when the response is that of the sole rival supplier, or one of only a few such rivals, that rival must be expected to know that he can powerfully affect our firm's affairs. What he will do will depend on his judgement of those effects, and that judgement, and the assumptions on which it is based, may be very hard for our firm to guess. Then in deciding on its own policy or action, firm A must reckon that firm B will be conscious of firm A's moves and will itself be considering how to anticipate or counter them. The difference between the situation of the oligopolist, the

135

member of a small group of suppliers of some rather insulated market, and that of one inconsiderable member of a vast group of competitors, is that the latter can count upon a passive response from buyers and the absence of express response from rivals, while the former must reckon on the alert, aggressive and calculating reaction of his competitors. The difference will evidently be a matter of degree, one situation will be assimilated by small steps to the other, and there will be cases which are hard to classify in one category or the other. But a theory which is to deal with the essence of the few-seller or two-seller situation (oligopoly or duopoly) will have to differ radically from the equilibrium conceptions we studied in Chapter 3.

Even more remote from those conceptions is the case of two parties, a buyer and a seller, bargaining face to face. F. Y. Edgeworth in his *Mathematical Psychics* reduced this situation to its barest essentials by considering Robinson Crusoe and Man Friday alone on their island seeking the terms on which Friday shall allow himself to be employed by Crusoe. Here, in the most literal sense, there is only one buyer and only one seller of the commodity, there is bilateral monopoly in the purest conceivable form. The case of a trade union leader who can withhold the labour of all his members *en bloc*, facing the representative of an association of all the potential employers, does not differ in essentials. In this chapter we wish to see what can be said about duopoly or oligopoly, and about bargaining or bilateral monopoly, the two types of situation where a decision-maker most explicitly and consciously bases his own choice of action on his suppositions about the equally conscious response of the other party. The two types have a peculiar logical paradox in common.

A theory of duopoly must ascribe to each of the two suppliers of a unified market for a uniform product some principle, not necessarily the same as his rival's, according to which he will decide what daily quantity to offer or what price per unit to charge. The market being unified, neither rival can sell at a higher price than the other and a single price will prevail. That price, reflecting the tastes of a mass of inter-competing buyers, will be a function of the quantity offered by both sellers taken together. The decision-principle adopted by each seller ought, therefore, to make some assumption about the character of the principle which will be adopted by the other. We say 'will be adopted', since it is the convention in analysis of duopoly to assume that the rivals with formal courtesy allow each other to make alternate moves. Augustin Cournot in 1838, in his great pioneering treatise on mathematical economics,[1] supposed each duopolist to assume, each time the move was his, that in total disregard of what that move should have proved to be, his opponent's output would

[1] *Recherches sur les principes mathématiques de la théorie des richesses.*

remain at the level it had attained before that move. In making this assumption duopolist 1 would be ascribing to his opponent quite different beliefs and reactions from his own, despite the perfect mutual symmetry of their respective situations. For duopolist 1 intends to *change* his own output to that size which, provided duopolist 2's output remains *unchanged*, will be most profitable.

Cournot's proposal ignores, not solves, the essential duopoly problem, for it supposes each rival to assume passivity on the part of the other in a situation whose whole point and essence is their inevitable awareness of the power of each to alter the conditions of the other's sales. Duopoly presents an extraordinary paradox, for in the purest case of symmetry between the two suppliers, it would appear quite arbitrary to ascribe to them different ideas about each other's likely actions. Yet if *each* makes, for example, the Cournot assumption, he will be basing his own action upon an error. Each rival's chosen action, if it is to be successful, must be based on expectations which are inconsistent with it.[2]

Duopoly defeats the methods of equilibrium analysis because equilibrium is the situation which reconciles the interests of fully informed participants who act by logic. In duopoly, the rightness of given conduct for one party depends on his assuming that the other party will adopt different conduct. But where is the logic or the ground for his making that assumption? Regular economic analysis assumes that men will pursue their interests by applying reason to complete relevant information. In duopoly, the information if available to one party is not available to the other, since its possession by both is a logical contradiction of its existence. Theory can say only that if the duopolists insist on behaving as duopolists, men seeking to out-manuvœre each other, they will engage in a series of mutually hostile moves the nature of whose beginning and end, from the viewpoint of the non-participant analyst, are arbitrary and unpredictable. An instinctive recognition of the futility or basic irrationality of pure duopolistic action may lead the parties to avoid that action. They may collude with each other and form a monopoly, thus making their joint net revenue as great as the market for their product allows and sharing this on some agreed rule. Or each may simply refrain from moving at all from the price at which he happens to be selling his product, for fear that the consequences would worsen his position which ever way he might move. The reasoning which would lead him to behave in this way is referred to as that of the kinky oligopoly demand-curve.

---

[2] See the admirably concise statement of the matter in Alan Coddington, *Theories of the Bargaining Process* (George Allen & Unwin, 1968), pp. 58 and following.

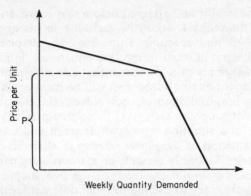

The kinky oligopoly demand curve. The oligopolist will hesitate to change his price from its prevailing level p, whatever that may be, for fear that his rivals will follow him down but not up.

FIG. 6.1

The duopolist or oligopolist, we suppose, finds himself charging for each unit of his product a price shown as p in Fig. 6.1. Shall he reduce this price in the hope that the elasticity of demand for his own output is great enough for the extra revenue to exceed the extra cost of production? The effect of such a price reduction on his revenue, we remember, will consist of the extra weekly quantity sold times the new price, minus the old weekly quantity sold times the reduction in price. Whether this effect will be an increase or decrease of net revenue depends on the elasticity of demand for his own product, when all the repercussions of his price change are taken into account. But those repercussions will include, so he fears, comparable price reductions on the part of his one or two rivals, who cannot fail to be noticeably affected in the first place by his action and will surely react to it. If all the rivals reduce their prices together, all will benefit only to the extent of the market elasticity of demand for their type of product, and this elasticity may well be judged by each of them insufficient to make a price reduction worth while. If our oligopolist could count on being left alone to reduce his price while rival prices stayed unchanged, he might hope to take away demand from his rivals. But this, he thinks, they will plainly not allow him to do. Thus he dare not reduce his price. Shall he raise it, in the belief that the elasticity of demand for his own output is so low that what he loses by reduction of quantity sold will be more than compensated by the higher price? Such a low elasticity depends on the supposition that his rivals will raise their prices with his. But if they do not, he may merely lose his market to them. Thus he dare not raise his price. The demand-curve facing a firm is, in such a case, a subjective judgement made by the firm. If the duopolist's reasoning runs on the lines we have described, the demand-curve facing him will be kinked at the prevailing price, having relatively high elasticity above that price and relatively low elasticity below it, and he will believe himself to be imprisoned at that price. Professor Kaldor's suggestion of the kinked oligopoly demand-curve thus accounts for a petrification of price in an industry of few sellers, which may last until some radical techno-logical innovation or change of consumer fashion suggests that individual firms can take profitable action on their own.

Duopoly differs from so-called bilateral monopoly in that the duopolists are not, so long as they remain duopolists, seeking to concert their action. By contrast, bilateral monopolists, that is, bargainers, are seeking terms for exchange between themselves. Their mutual dependence is of the essence of their situation. Bargaining is even more elusive to the equilibrium analyst than duopoly, for it involves not merely lack of knowledge but deliberately induced ignorance and false beliefs.

It was the search for a theory of bargaining that led Edgeworth to invent the concept of indifference-curve. He measures northwards from the origin the daily hours of work given by Man Friday, and eastwards from the origin the daily shillings of pay given by Crusoe. Any point in the north-eastern quadrant, up to the longest conceiv-able day's work, thus represents a contract between Friday and Crusoe to exchange so much work for so much pay. For each sup-posed amount of work there will be some amount of pay which would just and only just compensate Friday for that amount of work, and there will be some amount of pay, in general a different amount, which Crusoe would just and only just be willing to give for that amount of work. The points representing those hypothetical con-tracts to which Friday would barely consent form his indifference-curve. He is indifferent between signing and not signing any one of these contracts. For Crusoe there is a different curve where every point is neither better nor worse than not having any agreement at all. Not having any agreement at all is a state represented by the origin, from which accordingly both curves begin. For Friday one daily hour of work would be no hardship, and would buy him his most acutely needed goods, so if need be he would sell this hour cheap. At each greater contemplated number of hours, he will be more and more reluctant to add the fatigues and loss of leisure which one extra hour would entail, and less and less acutely in need of the goods which it would buy. Thus his indifference-curve will have a great deal of north near the origin, but more and more east as it reaches higher numbers of hours. His curve will be convex north–westwards. Crusoe will need the first hour of Friday's work very acutely, and later hours less so, while any given quantity of goods which he must sacrifice to buy an extra hour will mean more to him as the number of contemplated hours becomes greater and the pay leaves less and less goods for himself. Thus his curve will run very much eastwards at first and swing more and more northwards, and thus will be convex south-eastwards. Edgeworth's diagram of these two curves is shown in our Fig. 6.2.

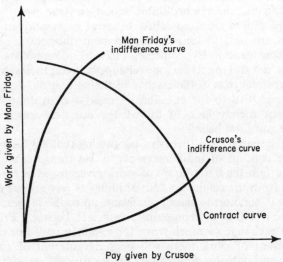

Edgeworth's bargaining diagram.

FIG. 6.2

For each of the bargainers, Edgeworth shows only one indifference-curve, namely that one where every point is equivalent, for that bargainer, to not having any contract at all. But Man Friday does wish to earn some money in exchange for work, and Crusoe to hire him, and there are terms which both will like better than having no contract. These points lie between the two indifference-curves. Through any one such point we can conceive a curve to be drawn which would contain all points equally valued with that point by one of the bargainers. This would be for him another indifference-curve, one on which every point would be preferred to any point on one of Edgeworth's own original curves. Every point in the whole region between the Edgeworthian curves would lie on one or other of an infinite family of such curves densely covering the whole region, and expressing the tastes of Man Friday, and every point would also lie

140

on one or other of a family of such curves expressing the tastes of Crusoe. How would these two families of curves be related? Evidently only one of Friday's indifference-curves would pass through the origin, since every point on every other curve represents a contract preferred to the no-contract situation. Thus Friday's curves would spring from points on the east–west axis eastward of the origin. Crusoe's similarly would start from points on the north–south axis northward of the origin, each desirable exchange of pay for work having, for Crusoe, some equivalent of a smaller amount of work for no pay. For the same reason that Friday's Edgeworth indifference-curve, passing through the origin, is convex north-westwards, so will be all his other indifference-curves. Likewise Crusoe's curves will be convex south-eastwards. We may reasonably speculate that there will be a series of points in each of which one curve of Friday's is tangent to one of Crusoe's, and that such tangencies will form an arc, convex to the north-east and stretching from one to the other of the Edgeworth indifference-curves. Edgeworth calls this segment or arc of tangencies the *contract-curve*. (see Fig. 6.3) Any point to the

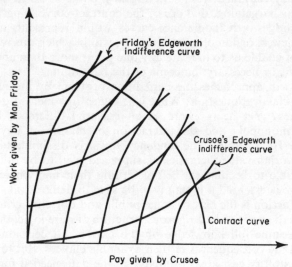

The contract curve as the locus of tangencies of a Friday indifference curve with a Crusoe indifference curve.

FIG. 6.3

north-eastward of the contract-curve will lie between a pair of curves, one of Friday's and one of Crusoe's, which converge to a tangency at the contract-curve. Thus from Crusoe's point of view, such a point will represent too much pay for a given quantity of work, and from Friday's point of view, too much work for a given amount of pay, *in comparison with the amounts represented by the tangency*. It is apparent also, that any such point lying outside the contract-curve will lie between infinitely many pairs of mutually tangential indifference-curves. Thus if Friday and Crusoe were to hit on such a point by way of starting their negotiation, both would be willing to move towards the contract-curve. By similar reasoning, if they were to hit on a starting point to the south-west of the contract-curve, both would be willing to move towards it from that direction, going, in this case, towards larger amounts of both pay and work. On the contract-curve itself, however, they would find themselves in disagreement over any proposal to move along the contract-curve, since evidently any such move would imply either more pay for less work or more work for less pay. Since both would be in agreement not to move off the contract-curve, they would find themselves immovably imprisoned on any point on the contract-curve which they might arbitrarily or randomly have hit upon as the starting-point of their bargaining. And if they refrained from selecting any point at all at which to begin their bargaining, that arc of the contract-curve lying between the two Edgeworth indifference-curves would represent, in Edgeworth's view, a region of indeterminacy, within which our reasoning would not enable us to indicate any one point more than another as the proper, or necessary, outcome of the bargaining.

Edgeworth approaches the bargaining problem by means of the pure neo-classical question: What is it logical for men to do, given their tastes? Yet he is aware of an essential difference between bilateral monopoly and the interaction of masses of buyers and suppliers. He refers to 'the tendency towards dissimulation'. The great Victorian value-theoreticians supposed men to be fully informed, or able to become so, before settling their final choices. Full knowledge is essential if a man is to be able to demonstrate that his choice of action is the best by some public and objective criterion. If economic theory is to be a rigorous structure of pure logic, therefore, it must assume full knowledge on the part of all decision-makers regarding the consequences of their available choices. But to assume this is to stultify vast areas of analysis. The data needed for insight into men's actions are the answers to the questions: What do they possess? (in material wealth and personal skills): What do they desire? and What do they know? In a face-to-face contest the knowledge possessed, or the beliefs or assumptions adopted, by one party and the other, are prime and dominating factors in shaping the result. And bargaining is a face-to-face contest. It is essential to disguise from the other party, as far as you can, what you are ultimately willing to do. The bargaining situation thus stands at the opposite pole from that of the equilibrating market, where, because of his insignificance, each individual is content to contribute his own mite of undissembled truth (his willingness to buy or supply such and such a quantity at such and such a price) and accept the solutions distilled from the combining of all such mites by the great market computer.

Let us suppose that Crusoe's and Friday's discussion comes to centre on some one point in that segment of the contract-curve which is bounded by their respective indifference-curves. As soon as both realize that they are discussing such a point, movement away from it will be impossible. For then each knows that the other will be better satisfied with that contract than with no contract at all, and will be better satisfied with that contract than with one which lies off the contract-curve. And having that knowledge, neither of them will presumably be willing to move along the curve in that sense which for him will lead to less favourable terms. But if, before any one point on the contract-curve is specially envisaged, Friday can persuade Crusoe that Friday's indifference-point lies more to the south-east than in fact it does, he will guard himself against a range of less favourable possibilities. And similarly if Crusoe can persuade Friday that Crusoe's indifference-point lies further north-west than it does, he will gain an advantage. Concealment and active deception are, as Edgeworth recognized with distaste, a part of the essence of bargaining. Edgeworth fastidiously turned aside from that aspect. We cannot fail to sympathize with his repugnance. Yet the fact is real and must be faced.

In so far as each bargainer recognizes that the other seeks to dissemble his real thoughts, each must suppose that the best he himself can do is to set limits in advance to the range of his own moves, and leave their precise character to depend on what his opponent does. To simplify our study of such bargaining policies, we shall suppose that only one variable, namely price, is to be settled between the bargainers, and that the quantity is a constant, or that the bargaining concerns the price of a single indivisible object. We need only consider one bargainer's policy in detail. The seller, for example is concerned with four levels of the price:

1. His absolute minimum price m, to accept which would only just compensate him for parting with the object which is being traded.
2. His gambit price, g, that is, the price he will announce at the outset.
3. His effective minimum price, j, the least that some chosen policy will allow him to accept.

4. The agreed price, v, at which, if at all, the object will change hands.

And with the following quantities composed from those prices:

5. His gain, $x = v - m$.
6. His descent, $s = g - v$.

Although we have assumed that the price of the traded object is the only variable explicitly under discussion between the bargainers, there is something else which either may have in mind. This is his own public character and prestige as a bargainer. If the present negotiation is deemed by him to be a unique or isolated incident in his life, he will be unconcerned with the impression he leaves of being tough or the opposite, of meaning what he says or of being ready to make bluffing suggestions. But if bargaining is his business or profession, he will be concerned to avoid *loss of face*. And this preoccupation may of course weigh more or less with him in comparison with the desire to conclude a bargain somewhere in his *contract zone*, that is, at a price which, apart from other considerations, makes the bargain preferable to having no contract at all. We accordingly distinguish three types of policy available to the seller:

1. He can resolve that, whatever price g he first asks, he will not reduce his subsequent asking prices so far as to diminish his prestige as a bargainer and so prejudice his standing in future negotiations. He will, if this course entails it, allow the negotiation to break down. This is the 'possible breakdown' policy.
2. He can resolve that, whatever g he first asks, he will subsequently make whatever concessions may be necessary to secure agreement, short of accepting a price less than m. This is the 'possible loss of face' policy.
3. He can resolve that the limit of his concessions shall depend on the particular g which he names. If agreement is not secured by concessions within this limit, he will allow the negotiation to break down. This is the 'combined policy'.

The task of each bargainer is to choose simultaneously a policy and an initial asking price, and if he chooses the combined policy, also an effective minimum price. Such a set of decisions, which we shall call a bargaining plan, must be thought of as a unified entity to be formed as a whole. The decisions cannot be taken independently of each other. One policy is not by itself better than another, nor one initial price better than another, but comparison must be between entire plans. Any such bargaining plan, like an investment plan, seems to contain possibilities of better or worse. The outcome of the negotiation cannot be known, but the chosen plan ought to be that which seems to bring within the range of possibility the finest outcome compatible with the exclusion of outcomes which would be disastrous or bad in an absolute sense. One means for representing such an uncertainty situation is by determining for each plan a focus gain and a focus loss in the sense in which these terms were defined in Chapter 4, and plotting each such pair on an appropriate form of indifference-map.

The seller's bargaining plan, we shall suppose, will be based on the degrees of possibility which he ascribes to hypotheses concerning the buyer's effective maximum price. The seller will be indifferent whether that price is the buyer's absolute maximum for a possible loss of face policy or the buyer's effective maximum for a possible breakdown policy. As the seller passes in review increasing levels at which he might set his own initial asking price, he must at the same time consider the corresponding effective minimum prices of his own which these asking prices entail. In the possible loss of face policy, these effective minimum prices will be all one and the same, and they will be his absolute minimum price. In the possible breakdown policy, they will depend on the initial asking price. The seller may conceive that the eventual agreed price, if any, will be an increasing function of his own initial asking price, provided he succeeds in judging for that initial price a level from which, within some chosen policy, he can descend as far as the buyer's effective maximum price. On this count, therefore, the seller has an incentive to try and set an initial asking price high enough to bring the eventual agreed price up to the buyer's effective maximum. Under a seller's possible breakdown policy, the seller has therefore simply to limit his initial price to that level whence a descent to the buyer's maximum is possible without loss of face. Since the buyer's maximum is not, in the seller's mind, a single numerical value but a range, to whose values the seller ascribes various degrees of possibility (or of potential surprise), the seller may find his focus gain in an agreed price carrying, in the seller's mind, some less than perfect possibility. Under the possible loss of face policy, the seller need not limit his initial asking price to any defined distance above the buyer's supposed maximum. But as he increases this distance (in the course of his mental review of plans) he must deduct from the gain $g - m$ corresponding to each higher level of g, an increasing allowance, translated into spot cash terms, for the entailed loss of face.

On what ground is this translation to be made? 'Loss of face' means simply impairment of future bargaining power, that is, it means loss of *future* possible gains. The nature of the two opposite policies, of possible breakdown and of possible loss of face, is that while each of them seeks immediate gain, one does so by risking immediate loss, the other by risking future loss. In order to assess in spot cash the loss of face entailed by any given descent $g-v$ from any given g, the bargainer must have in mind some conception of the numbers, importance and time-distribution of his future bargaining encounters, and in principle he ought evidently to discount the gains, whose possibility in such future negotiations he is proposing to sacrifice, at the prevailing market interest rate for their respective deferments. Plainly such refinements will in practice be swept away in favour of a purely intuitive or instinctive 'feel' for the value of a tough bargaining reputation.

What, under each policy, does the seller stand to lose? The opportunity-cost of adopting the possible breakdown policy is plainly the sacrifice of the best hope he could have entertained under the possible loss of face policy, it is the hope of that gain which, having regard both to its size and to the ease or difficulty of believing it attainable, is the most attractive possibility held out by the possible loss of face policy, it is in fact the focus gain of this alternative policy. Under the possible loss of face policy, his loss of face may in the end outweigh in his estimation any gain $v-m$ which he achieves, and the net loss thus resulting from both considerations taken together will be the focus loss of this policy. All these quantities, let us remind ourselves, are *ex ante* conceptions in the mind of the bargainer, passed in review as he decides upon his plan. Under the 'combined' policy there will be, for each given initial asking price, a different focus loss for each different effective minimum price. A particular pair of values of g and j being specified, the bargainer will assign some degree of possibility to the hypothesis that with this g and this j the negotiation will break down and thus involve him in the combined loss consisting of the loss of face due to the descent $g-j$ plus the sacrifice of the focus gain of the most attractive plan under the 'possible loss of face' policy. Thus under the 'combined' policy each different plan, consisting of a different g or a different j, or both, will have in principle its own distinct pair of focus gain or focus loss. When the seller has passed in review what he deems a sufficient range of plans under each of the policies, and has provided each plan with its focus gain and loss, these pairs of focus outcomes can, in principle, be compared with each other by means of his bargainer-indifference map and the one which best satisfies him thus selected. We have been speaking of the seller, but the buyer's problem is the same in nature, *mutatis mutandis*.

The positions of the two bargainers before the beginning of any interchange of offers are essentially symmetrical. Which of them is the first to announce a price may affect the course and ultimate result of the bargaining, for it may be necessary for either party to choose a fresh bargaining plan any number of times in the course of the negotiation. Each successive asking price named by the seller is a new piece of information for the buyer. It may fit perfectly into his previous conception of what was in the seller's mind, or it may compel a complete refashioning of his own ideas. On our assumptions, however, the seller's asking price and the buyer's offered price will move towards each other. If we knew precisely what inferences each would draw from any given move of the other, and if we had full knowledge of the tastes of each as expressed by his bargainer indifference map, we could conceptually determine at what price agreement or breakdown would be reached.

The analysis we have outlined leads to two conclusions in conflict with those of Edgeworth and the many others who have followed him in concentrating in this matter on the sole question of what the bargainers desire to the exclusion of the question of what they know or believe. Edgeworth concluded that the existence of a contract zone, a range of prices within which agreement would benefit both parties, would ensure that such an agreement would be attained, but that within that zone, we had no means of saying what particular price would be agreed upon. We have concluded that when uncertainty is given its full role, and when a series of possible future occasions of bargaining are considered, the existence of a contract-zone does not in itself guarantee an agreement, but that the result, whether agreement or breakdown, is in some sense determinate. Perhaps the main inference which ought to be drawn by the economic theoretician from his study of bargaining is the crippling and misleading effect upon his analysis of a neglect of the question of what people can know and how they can come by their knowledge. Edgeworth was perfectly aware of this problem in general, as his invention of the idea of re-contact, to explain the working of a competitive market, testifies. But the discovery of the indifference-curve and of the contract-curve were surely inventions enough for one piece of analysis.

CHAPTER 7

Profit and Equilibrium

1. POLICY, SURPRISE AND DECISION

Equilibrium means in economics the best momentary adjustment to existing circumstances. It is a definition which plainly has many implications and raises many questions. For the theoretician, one addendum is vital. 'Circumstances' must be qualified by 'so far as they are known'. To forget that the business of living, and within that larger whole, the business of producing and exchanging goods, essentially and inescapably involves and requires the continuous and endless gaining of knowledge, is to divorce our theories from half their subject matter. To say that there is always potential new knowledge to be gained is to say that possessed knowledge is always incomplete, unsure and potentially wrong. Part of the state of adjustment to circumstances as they are known, which constitutes equilibrium, ought therefore to be a moral and intellectual readiness to adjust the knowledge itself according to the out-turn of seeking to apply it. All is experiment.

Systematic activity needs a purpose and a policy. A policy is a set of principles. It seeks to classify situations and to classify courses of action, and to do these things in such a way that for any class of situations a class of appropriate courses is suggested. A policy must therefore be capacious enough, 'open-minded' enough, to cope with anything that seems able to distil itself from history's bubbling cauldron. A policy needs to be such that widely various things can occur which will not disconcert it. So long as what occurs is provided for by the policy which is in force, action is mere administration. Judgement is still called for, to place each emerging stage of the evolution of affairs in its proper division of the filing system and to select the class of response which the policy indicates. Further, within that class of response the exact character of the move to be made remains at the discretion of the man in charge. There is need and scope here also for skill and resource. If we wish, we may call such reactions 'decisions'. But there is a weightier meaning for which this word ought possibly to be reserved. The policy itself can fail. It can prove manifestly less apt to actuality than had been expected. It can plainly be failing to take advantage of newly apparent openings, or it can be making bad outcomes worse. The outcome of what the firm, for example, has done can be so different from anything that was reckoned on, that the policy is at a loss. Policy itself must then be reformed. *Decision* ought perhaps to mean the invention of new policies, even policies that were beyond the mind's reach, that were logically non-existent, with the knowledge formerly possessed. Decision, in the origin of this word, means an act of cutting, and it is the appropriate and precise word for the psychic act of cutting the future from the past, for discarding the existing policy and many of its preconceptions in favour of novelties and unfamiliar implications. We need a measure of the power to induce a transformation of policy, which can be exercised by a surprising consequence of existing policy. Within the confines of our subject matter, such a measure can be found in the elasticity of surprise.

Elasticity of surprise is applicable only to those departures from the expected which we shall call counter-expected events. For departures from the expected can be of either of two kinds. A hypothetical event or class of events can have been envisaged and excluded, can have been dismissed in the sense of being assigned a high degree of potential surprise. The actual occurrence of such an event would then occasion great surprise, and ought to be the signal for reconsideration of the whole system of assumptions on which high potential surprise had been assigned to it. But the over-turn of assumptions and beliefs would be greater still, if the actual event were of a character which had in no way entered into any reckoning or been even remotely imagined. The former class we may call counter-expected events, the latter class unexpected events. 'Events' which are defined merely by the naming of a value for a single variable can perhaps only fall into the counter-expected class. For in assigning degrees of potential surprise to values of a single variable, the whole range of that variable, logically conceivable under the most abstract conditions, is implicitly considered. It is when events consist of complex configurations involving many variables, or even qualitative rather than measurable characteristics, that the possibility of the totally unexpected event comes in. An event which appears unrelated to one's frame of thought, to which no bearings can be assigned and for which no origin or natural genesis can be perceived (an event such as the observation of phenomena contrary to received natural laws) must necessarily call in question any system of expectations formerly held or reduce it to disorder. Counter-expected events, and *a fortiori* unexpected events, bring existing policies into disrepute and essentially render them obsolete. It is in the nature of the case difficult to place any limits in advance on the consequences of an unexpected event, since such an event is defined as something not previously conceived. But it is in principle possible for the contriver of a policy to outline in advance his response to a counter-expected event. That response will depend quantitatively on the degree to which the event departs from expectation. In our context such preparation can be illustrated by plans which a businessman may make to extend further the scale of a plant which he now has it in mind to build, in case his market proves larger than he now thinks feasible. The proportionate change in the scale of action of some kind, foreseen in such advance contingency planning, in relation to the proportion in which the counter-expected outcome has diverged from expectation, is what we mean by the elasticity of surprise.

2. ELASTICITIES OF SURPRISE

We have defined *investment-gain* as the excess of a businessman's valuation of some plant which he has it in mind to construct, over the cost of that construction. His valuation of the plant will depend on his conjectures concerning the trading revenues it will earn in each future year or other unit interval. Thus the investment-gain itself is evidently conjectural, and will be a typical example, within the business field, of those variables for which a decision-maker may wish to form a potential surprise function, neutral value and ascendancy surface so as to arrive at focus values. If the plant is in fact constructed, the lapse of time during its working life will bring changes in the value placed upon it, at any stage of this life, by the businessman. Wear and tear will tend to reduce its value, technological progress may bring nearer the time of its obsolescence. But the course of these successive revaluations will also depend on the course of the recorded trading revenues which are actually earned. The trading revenue of any interval which is still in the future can have in the businessman's mind its own function assigning degrees of potential surprise to various hypotheses of its size, concerning which he can thus have in mind a neutral value and upper and lower focus values. We shall confine our attention to the upper focus value of the trading revenue of some named (dated) interval, and the excess g of this upper focus trading revenue over the neutral revenue. It may be reasonable to suppose that when the recorded trading revenue for any just-elapsed interval lies between the neutral value and the upper focus value, the business man's valuation of the plant will remain unchanged. But when the recorded revenue exceeds, let us say by Δg, the focus-hypothesis which he has been assigning to it, we may suppose that his valuation of the plant, and accordingly his view of the investment gain which he will ultimately have realized at the end of the plant's life, will be revised upwards. Let us write j for the focus investment-gain which he has hitherto entertained, and $j + \Delta j$ for the new focus investment gain resulting from his revision of expectations due to the excess Δg of recorded trading revenue over its former upper focus-value. Then we mean by *valuation elasticity of surprise* the expression

$$\frac{\Delta j}{j} \bigg/ \frac{\Delta g}{g} \quad \text{or} \quad \frac{g}{j} \frac{\Delta j}{\Delta g}$$

Such a change in the businessman's assessment of his existing plant (as compared with what his valuation of it would have been, at this stage of its life, if recent trading revenue had fallen within its own inter-focal range) may induce a change in his intentions for further investment in plant. If his intended investment in the *impending* interval is raised from I_n to $I_n + \Delta I_n$, we may refer to the ratio $\Delta I_n / I_n : \Delta j / j$ as the *investment elasticity of surprise for valuation*, and to the ratio $\Delta I_n / I_n : \Delta g / g$ as the *investment elasticity of surprise for trading revenue*. It is plain that these three elasticities will be very simply related arithmetically, since we have

$$\frac{g}{I_n} \frac{\Delta I_n}{\Delta g} = \frac{j}{I_n} \frac{\Delta I_n}{\Delta j} \frac{g}{j} \frac{\Delta j}{\Delta g}$$

Such concepts may be somewhat remote from the businessman's usual modes of thought, but they might serve, if he were to incorporate them into his outfit of thought-tools, to bring some extra clarity into his decision-making, by which we are proposing to mean his policy-reconstructing.

3. EQUILIBRIUM AND THE UNKNOWN

Our theme in this book has been the nature and origin of the firm's production policy. We sought broad insight into the firm's mode of answering its policy questions: what to produce, in what quantities per time unit, and by what technological use of what means. Policy springs from purpose, and we defined the firm's purpose as the making as large as possible, within its circumstances, of the excess of the value of its outputs over that of its inputs; and the pursuit of this aim, not merely in the short period when its circumstances were largely given, but with a long perspective of time when those circumstances could themselves be modified and in some degree chosen. In the older language of economic theory, this system of objectives and guiding considerations could have been called the pursuit of profit. However, we have found the matter of defining 'the excess of the value of outputs over that of inputs' to be a complex one. Above all, we have been confronted with one major and inescapable difficulty. Action can only be framed in the light of such knowledge as we possess, and that knowledge is in the nature of things insufficient, since it necessarily excludes much of those future circumstances whose character will determine the outcome of whatever we now do or decide. Profit is thus not a single and simple idea but a system of concepts, and our final purpose is to arrange them in a scheme or array to summarize that system.

Most essential of all is the distinction between things expected and things recorded. Things recorded cannot in themselves be changed, though we may revise our measurements and judgements of them. They cannot, therefore, in themselves be the objectives of policy. Policy is concerned with things looked forward to. But the situation from which we start to seek those objectives is given, it is *the present in the sense of the immediate past*. The immediate past, too, is largely carried forward from an earlier past. Thus what has happened largely shapes what can happen, what can be done within a shorter or longer stretch of time to come. Moreover, the way things happen can only be learnt from the way things have happened. Even at its best and most complete, the knowledge of the way things have happened may still leave us in the dark. There is novelty. The chemist, it is said, has as yet no means of knowing fully what properties will be possessed by the compound he is about to synthesize, from a knowledge of the properties of its composing elements. But such knowledge as we have is knowledge of the past.

The scheme of profit-ideas, therefore, must include both recorded and expected quantities, and especially it must distinguish between these categories. It is only in special cases, by means of special arrangements such as legal contract, that the need to keep the two ideas separate can sometimes be neglected. *Expectation of profit* must be provided with a language for expressing its uncertainty and its dual resulting character of threat and promise, and this language must be such that a precise subjective comparison can be made, *ex post facto*, between the system of expectations and the recorded result, so as to indicate the response that will or should be made. The system of profit-ideas, that is to say, is required to express the grounds of stability, or of rejection and renewal, of policy. Policy will be stable, so long as profit proves to be what was, in some sense, expected. In what sense?

By *expectation* we have proposed to mean the adjudgement of possibility, that is to say, the adjudgement of a degree of conformity or compatibility with two sets of conditions, the general nature and mode of operation of the world, and its particular state at the moment when expectations are being formed. A situation, or a transform of one situation into another (an 'event') will be adjudged in some degree possible if it does not conflict with general 'laws', 'principles' or stereotypes which are accepted by the expectation former by reason of his personal fortuitous experience or his systematic study of things; and if the imagined situation or event is sufficiently deferred from this present moment of expectation-forming, for the present situation to have time to be transformed into the imagined one. How much time needs to be allowed will again, of course, be a judgement of the expectation former, based on his beliefs about the speed at which things can change and perhaps, at a higher level of subtlety, about the acceleration which this speed seems to be undergoing.

Decision seems to us to be a psychic act engendered by *feelings about thoughts*. The thoughts involved, in our context, are those which specify sizes of gain or loss and which associate degrees of possibility with these sizes. It will be a source of extra efficiency if the statement of degrees of possibility can already be made in terms of feeling, and we have proposed to effect this by expressing them as potential surprise. A dated future situation, or transform of situations, will on this view be assigned zero potential surprise if the expectation former has in mind *no contrary evidence or adverse considerations*. Possibility is thus distinguished from probability by being an expression of the absence of (intellectual, subjective) impediments, in the thought of the expectation former. By *an expectation* we mean a specific size of gain or loss associated with a given degree of potential surprise or possibility. It is thus a vector of two elements. Each of these elements is to be regarded, we think, as an independent variable governing the degree of ascendancy of the expectation, its power to arrest the expectation former's attention in his process of arriving at a decision to invest, or not, in the particular plant.

Within this scheme of ideas, one important meaning of profit, or one important concept coming within the skein of profit-ideas, is, thus the pair of focus outcomes ascribed to any investment project, those sizes of hypothetical investment gain or loss whose respective degrees of ascendancy are greater than those of other hypotheses. When the notion of focus outcomes is applied to the trading revenue of some named calendar interval (an interval which, perhaps, represents only a small part of the assumed economic life of an existing plant), it is these outcomes which perhaps can serve as the bounds within which the recorded out-turn of that interval must fall if the businessman is to regard his expectation system as having been vindicated in respect of that interval. If the recorded out-turn falls outside these bounds, the excess of recorded gain over focus gain, or the numerical excess of recorded loss over focus loss, is another meaning of profit, or another profit-idea, which must be included in our scheme of profit-ideas. We have proposed above, to base upon the comparison of this counter-expected profit with the 'expected' or focus profit, the concepts of valuation-elasticity of surprise and investment-elasticity of surprise.

The recorded out-turn of a succession of past intervals has, of course, its own effect upon affairs and, in particular, on the business-man's conduct, in other ways than by inducing him to retain or replace his policy or his plant. For these out-turns affect the quantity of his investible resources.

Equilibrium names a more coherent skein or system of ideas than profit. This system is the key to the whole of Western economics. It epitomizes the entire method, logic and conclusions of the economics that derives from Adam Smith, and is simply the working out of the consequences of a single supposition: that men seek to attain their desired results by applying reason to their known circumstances. Their conduct, it thus says, is governed by their desires and their resources. Their method of regulating the interaction of many men's independent desires is by exchange, since this gives everyone far more than he could achieve in isolation. Private property is a neces-sary supposition of this method, and the distribution of the total resources amongst individuals and nations is accepted as an accident of blind and impartial history, which must, however, be heavily modified in order that the strains of envy or desperation may not destroy the system. Traditionally, the equilibrium analysis has solved only half of the most intractable problem which confronts it: that of how men know what their circumstances, resources and opportuni-ties are. Equilibrium itself, in its strictest and most encompassing sense, is precisely designed to cope with as much of this problem as is capable of solution by logic. For it shows a means by which men can know, when each makes his own choice, what are the choices that other men are at that moment making. That knowledge is essential to rational individual choice, for the choices made by others, determining their actions and the use they will make of the means they possess, is part of the circumstances of each individual. Equilibrium solves the dilemma of concomitant choice (the dilemma that not everyone can choose last) by supposing that the choices of different individuals are pre-reconciled by the market. It is, however, only simultaneous choices that can be pre-reconciled. If any choice is deferred, that constitutes a gap in the complete knowledge on which complete rationality of conduct depends. And all of us are all the time deferring our choices. We are enabled effectively to do so by the institution of money, which inevitably by its nature enables a man to sell a particular, specialized object in exchange for a generalized claim on goods whose character he is not obliged then to specify. All men produce things, but they only decide whether to buy each other's products when it suits them, after those goods are made or much has been invested in their making. Modern business depends on the exploitation of the unknown. It is by a successful technological or commercial gamble that one firm gains an advantage over its rivals, and this advantage lasts only so long as it takes those rivals to imitate the product, method or market. To hit upon something new that will beat what exists is the only way for a firm to alter its rating in the table of success. Whether the society which depends on such a principle, the principle of actively and deliberately rendering obsolete as much of other people's work as one can as fast as one can, is a good or a stable society, is a question which history will answer in due course. Meanwhile, by what posture or policy can conduct within such a society claim to be apt and efficient?

To attempt some answer to this question, we have in the preceding pages invoked the ideas of *horizon* (the limitation of the time-range of attempted picturing of future outcomes), of *discounting* (the lesser valuation of more deferred and therefore more uncertain outcomes), of *ascendancy* (the balancing of greater imaginable gain or loss against increasing difficulty of imagining their reality), and of *liquidity* (the foregoing of specialized adaptation of some resources in favour of a reserve of general purchasing power). The application of ascendancy is to determine a 'worst' and 'best' outcome of each proposed course of action, in order to reject courses whose (subjectively) possible bad outcomes would be ruinous and to choose, amongst the others, the ones which seem to expose the firm to the most dramatic successes. Modern advance in business method consists largely in a continuous increase in the scope and rapidity of search in the field of conceivable courses of action. No such course can be examined until it has been imagined. Business 'research and development' is in essence *systematized imagination*. The computer has immensely increased the speed at which the process of examination of the true nature and implications of what has been conceived can be carried through, *so far as that examination can go*. Logic can be applied to problems of cost and revenue, of minimizing the one and maximizing the other, so long as those problems are formulated *as if* we knew all that we need to know. The paradox of business, in its modern evolution, is the conflict between our assumption that we know enough for our logic to bite on, and our *essential*, prime dependence on achieving *novelty*, the novelty which by its nature and meaning in some degree discredits what had passed for knowledge.

Index

156